# Old Bradford

## Paul Chrystal

Town Hall Square in the early 1960s.

## Stenlake Publishing Ltd

© 2023 Paul Chrystal
First Published in the United Kingdom, 2023
Stenlake Publishing Limited
54-58 Mill Square, Catrine, KA5 6RD
01290 551122
www.stenlake.co.uk

ISBN 978-1-84033-889-8

Printed by
P2D Books, 1 Newlands Rd,
Westoning, Bedford MK45 5LD

# BY THE SAME AUTHOR:

Bradford at Work
Bradford: Unique Images from the Archives of Historic England
Old Saltaire and Shipley
Leeds in 50 Buildings
Leeds's Military Legacy
Central Leeds Through Time
Leeds Central History Tour
The Place Names of Yorkshire

Huddersfield Through Time
Huddersfield History tour
The Confectionery Industry in Yorkshire
Yorkshire Literary Landscapes
Yorkshire Murders, Manslaughter, Madness & Executions
Yorkshire's Days of Steam
Haworth Timelines
Old Bramley & Stanningley

Ivegate .

# BRADFORD

When William I invaded England in 1066 Bradford folk were not best pleased. So, five years later they, like many others, did something about it and revolted; it was now William's turn to be displeased: he unleashed on Bradford what has become known, rather euphemistically, as the Harrying of the North – William's special brand of harrying resulted in the total devastation of the Bradford settlement, as recorded in Domesday. To make matters even worse, the emerging township then became part of the Honour of Pontefract and was gifted to Ilbert de Lacy for service to the Conqueror; there it stayed until 1311 after which the manor then passed through the Earl of Lincoln, John of Gaunt and The Crown, only reverting to private ownership in 1620.

In the meantime Bradford had become a small town clustered around Kirkgate, Westgate and Ivegate. There was a fulling mill, a soke mill where all the manor corn was milled and a market in 1316. During the Wars of the Roses Bradfordians allied with the House of Lancaster. Edward IV granted the right to hold two annual fairs and thenceforth the town was on the up. During Henry VIII's reign Bradford overtook Leeds as a manufacturing centre and over the next two centuries Bradford kept growing in line with the burgeoning woollen trade.

The Parliamentarians garrisoned Bradford during the Civil War and in 1642 it was unsuccessfully attacked by Royalist forces from Leeds. Sir Thomas Fairfax took command of the garrison and marched to do battle with the Duke of Newcastle but was defeated. The Parliamentarians retreated back to Bradford while the Royalists established headquarters at Bolling Hall from where the town was besieged, leading to its surrender. The Civil War had a depressing effect on industrial output but after the accession of William III and Mary II in 1689 things picked up again. The early 18th century saw a surge in manufacturing and the start of the town's modern development while new canal and turnpike road links boosted trade.

By 1801 Bradford was a rural market town of some 6,393 people; wool spinning and cloth weaving was rife in local cottages and farms. Bradford, though, was little bigger than Keighley (5,745) and was significantly smaller than Halifax (8,866) and Huddersfield (7,268). Bradford in effect was a hub for three nearby townships – Manningham, Bowling and Great and Little Horton, which were still separated from the town by green fields.

Things really began to change in 1788 when blast furnaces were established by Hird, Dawson, Hardy at Low Moor. Iron was worked by the Bowling Iron Company until about 1900. Yorkshire iron had a myriad of uses, including shackles, hooks and piston rods for locomotives, colliery cages and other mining appliances where strength was required. The Low Moor Company also made pig iron, employing 1,500 men in 1929. Around 1850 there were 46 coal mines within the town's boundaries. Coal output continued to expand, reaching a peak in 1868 when Bradford contributed 20% of all the coal and iron produced in Yorkshire, from 46 pits.

In 1841 the population of the township in 1841 was 34,560. The year 1847 was the year when the municipal borough of Bradford was created.

By the middle of the 19th century there were 38 worsted mills in Bradford town and 70 in the borough; it is estimated that two-thirds of the country's wool production was being processed in Bradford. Less than ten years later, Bradford had become the wool capital of the world.

As in other parts of the country, industrial and social unrest erupted from time to time. 1837 saw serious anti-Poor Law riots with operatives clashing with the 15th Hussars; when the Chartists drilled on Fairweather Green in 1839 they caused a riot. In 1842 there were plug-drawing riots (the 1842 General Strike) when Chartists mobilised resistance to wage cuts in the mills, spreading to involve nearly half a million workers throughout Britain and turning into the

William Edward Kilburn (1818 – 1891). View of the Great Chartist Meeting on Kennington Common (1848) Daguerreotype. In the Royal Collection; purchased by Prince Albert; one of a pair of daguerreotypes.

biggest single demonstration of working class strength in the 19th century. 1844 saw Orange disturbances with five protestors charged with manslaughter. On May 29th 1848 the new mayor was forced to call out the dragoons, police and special constables to suppress more Chartist agitation which led to many injuries. Bradford was 'in a state of siege'.

Back in the mills in 1825 the wool-combers union called a strike that lasted five months but workers were forced to return to work through hardship, leading to the introduction of machine-combing. This resulted in rapid growth, with wool imported in vast quantities for the manufacture of worsted cloth in which Bradford specialised, and the town soon became known as the wool capital of the world – Worstedopolis, just as Middlesbrough was Ironopolis. A permanent military presence was established in the city with the completion of Bradford Moor Barracks in 1844.

In 1890 the United States imposed a tariff on foreign cloth which led to a slashing of wages throughout the British textile industry. A strike in Bradford ensued, the Manningham Mills strike, which produced as a by-product the Bradford Labour Union, an organisation which sought to function politically independently of either the Whigs or the Tories. This initiative was replicated by others in Colne Valley, Halifax, Huddersfield and Salford. Such developments showed that working-class support for separation from the Liberal Party was growing in strength.

At a TUC meeting in September 1892, a call was issued for a meeting of advocates of an independent labour organisation. An arrangements committee was established and their conference was held in Bradford on 14th to 16th January 1893 at the Bradford Labour Institute, operated by the Labour Church. It turned out to be the foundation conference of the Independent Labour Party and MP Keir Hardie was elected as its first chairman.

About 130 delegates were at the conference, including author George Bernard Shaw, and Edward Aveling, son-in-law of Karl Marx. Some 91 local branches of the Independent Labour Party were represented, joined by eleven local Fabian Societies, and four branches of the Social Democratic Federation.

This mural is on the side of the Bradford Playhouse. It was painted in 1993 and commemorates the 100th anniversary of the founding, in Bradford, of the Independent Labour Party, the forerunner of our modern Labour Party.

Over the years there has been a number of eminent Bradfordians who have done much to improve social welfare, workers' rights and benefits and living conditions, not just in the immediate Bradford region but, ultimately in Great Britain generally. Titus Salt was one of these men; in 1833 he took over the running of his father's woollen business specialising in fabrics combining alpaca, mohair, cotton and silk. By 1850 he had five mills. However, because of the polluted environment and squalid conditions his workers had to endure and tired of the pig-headed apathy of his industrial competitors Salt left Bradford and moved his business to Salts Mill in Saltaire in 1850, where in 1853 he began to build the workers' village which has become a UNESCO World Heritage site. Another was Henry Ripley – a younger contemporary of Titus Salt. He was managing partner of Edward Ripley & Son Ltd, which owned the Bowling Dye Works. In 1880 the dye works employed over 1000 people and was said to be the biggest dye works in Europe. Like Salt he was a councillor, JP and Bradford MP who was passionate about improving working-class housing conditions. He built the industrial model village of Ripley Ville on a site in Broomfields, East Bowling, close to the dye works.

In 1914 the 22nd Annual Conference was held in Bradford as were the 1943 Jubilee Annual Conference and the 1954 62nd Annual Conference.

Bradford had always been troubled by bad drainage; the critical shortage of water in Bradford Dale was a serious brake on industrial expansion and improvement in urban sanitary conditions. In 1854 Bradford Corporation bought the Bradford Water Company and embarked on a huge engineering programme to bring supplies of soft water from Airedale, Wharfedale and Nidderdale. By 1882 water supply had radically improved when remedial waterworks in the Wharfedale scheme were completed; there was much to celebrate.

Bradford had ample supplies of locally-mined coal to provide the power that local industry needed. The deposits of sandstone were perfect raw material for building the mills, and with a population of 182,000 by 1850, the town grew rapidly as workers were attracted by jobs in the growing number of textile mills. Meanwhile, urban expansion took place along the routes out of the city towards the Hortons and Bowling; the townships had become part of a contiguous urban area by the late 19th century.

Some of Bradford's atrocious housing

Samuel Lister and his brother were major industrialists who were worsted spinners and manufacturers at Lister's Mill (also known as Manningham Mills); they were the epitome of Victorian enterprise and characterised everything the Industrial Revolution was about.

But the proliferation of steel and wool works came at a price. Bradford was a veritable hell hole of pollution. Rapid industrial growth brought with it over 200 factory chimneys persistently belching out black, choking sulphurous smoke; apart from what this did to the hearts and lungs of the population there were frequent outbreaks of cholera and typhoid, and only 30% of children born to textile workers reached the age of fifteen. This alarmingly high level of infant and youth mortality meant that anyone living in Bradford could look forward to a life expectancy of just over eighteen years – one of the lowest in the country.

George Weerth, the German writer friend of Marx and Engels, in between researching the impact of the Industrial Revolution on the relationship between property owners and the workers, earned a living in Bradford as a representative for a textile firm. In 1846 he vividly described the town in *Neue Rheinische Zeitung* as follows:

> Every other factory town in England is a paradise in comparison to this hole. In Manchester the air lies like lead upon you; in Birmingham it is just as if you were sitting with your nose in a stove pipe; in Leeds you have to cough with the dust and the stink as if you had swallowed a pound of Cayenne pepper in one go – but you can put up with all that. In Bradford, however, you think you have been lodged with the devil incarnate. If anyone wants to feel how a poor sinner is tormented in Purgatory, let him travel to Bradford.

The Bowling Iron Works adding to the pollution hell.

Looking down on Lister's Mill

From the mid-19th century, like many major cities, Bradford has acted as a magnet for immigrants. In the 1840s Bradford's population was significantly swollen by an influx of migrants from Ireland, particularly rural Mayo and Sligo, fleeing the Great Potato Famine and the depravations it, and the English government, were causing ; by 1851 about 10% of the Bradford population had been born in Ireland, the largest proportion in Yorkshire. Around the middle of the 19th century the Irish were concentrated in eight densely-settled areas situated near the town centre. One of these was the Bedford Street area of Broomfields which in 1861 supported 1,162 people of Irish birth—19% of all Irish-born persons in the Borough.

During the 1820s and 1830s, there was immigration from Germany. Many were Jewish merchants who invested large sums of money constructing imposing warehouses used mainly in the stuff trade for the storage and sale of their goods for export. Unsurprisingly, Germany was a particularly strong market for yarns and other textile goods, and several German shipping houses set up

An example of how Pakistani immigration has enriched Bradford society, adding an exotic flavour to an otherwise lacklustre Lumb Lane.

The Wool Exchange in Little Germany

their businesses in the area; other exporters were, for example, Thornton, Homan and Company in 1871 who traded with China and North America.

The 100 or so families which made up the German Jewish community congregated largely in the Manningham area, hence the name Little Germany. The architecture here is predominantly neoclassical with an Italian flavour. These unique structures form a collection of 85 buildings constructed between 1855 and 1890, of which 55 are listed. Bradford became more attractive as a centre of international trade in the aftermath of the Franco-Prussian War, which obviously disrupted commercial relations between France and Germany. So, the German Jews took an active role in the commercial prosperity of the town as well as contributing much to Bradford's civic life and culture.

Charles Semon (1814–1877) was a textile merchant and philanthropist who developed a productive textile export house in the town. Jacob Behrens (1806–1889) was the first foreign textile merchant to export woollen goods from Bradford; his company developed into an international multimillion-pound business. Behrens too was a philanthropist; he helped to establish the Bradford Chamber of Commerce in 1851. Jacob Moser (1839 – 1922) was a textile merchant who was a partner in the firm Edelstein, Moser and Co, which evolved into a successful Bradford textile export house. Moser was yet another philanthropist, and founded the Bradford Charity Organisation Society and the City Guild of Help.

Other industries included manufacturing companies making machinery to support the textile mills. The Jowett Motor Company was a prestigious motor car company, operating from Bradford from 1901 to 1954, thus spanning the golden age of British motor car production. The company was founded in 1901 by two brothers: Benjamin (1877–1963) and William (1880–1965) Jowett, together with Arthur V. Lamb. In the very early days the company focused on transport of the two-wheeled variety, taking advantage of the contemporary craze for bicycles and cycling. V-twin engines for driving machinery followed and some of these early engines found their way in the Bradford area into other makes of cars as replacement parts. In 1904 the name changed to the Jowett Motor Manufacturing Company based in Back Burlington Street. The first Jowett light car prototype emerged in February 1906; however, as the workshop was already busied with general engineering work, experiments with different engine configurations, and with manufacturing the first six Scott motorbikes, the inaugural model did not go into production until 1910, after more than 25,000 miles of exhaustive trials.

A 1937 Jowett 2 Ten 4-cylinder.

In the First World War the factory was converted to munitions manufacture. After the Armistice, in 1919, a new site was bought at Springfield Works, Bradford Road, Idle, on the site of a disused quarry.

The Scott Motorcycle Company was founded by Alfred Angas Scott in 1908 as the Scott Engineering Company and was owned by Scott Motors (Saltaire) Limited, Shipley. Scott motorcycles were made up to 1978. Perfecting the two stroke motorcycle engine was Scott's ambition: his early experiments with a two-stroke were in a motor boat; his first attempt on a motorcycle was when he fitted an engine he had designed to a Premier bicycle in 1901. He had already patented an early form of caliper brakes in 1897, a fully triangulated frame, and rotary induction valves. He invented the kick start. A vertical twin two-stroke engine came in 1908 featuring a 450 cc two-stroke twin-cylinder water-cooled engine. The first few machines were produced by Jowett in 1908; not long after, he set up as a manufacturer at the Mornington Works, Grosvenor Road in Bradford.

Bradford means in Old English the Broad Ford, a reference to a crossing of the Bradford Beck at Church Bank where a settlement grew in Saxon times. Domesday has it as "Bradeford". Bradford has a population of 536,986, which makes it the seventh-largest city in the United Kingdom and the third-largest city in Yorkshire and the Humber, after Leeds and Sheffield.

Much more on Bradford industry and commerce can be found in my *Bradford at Work* (2018); more on Saltaire in my *Old Saltaire and Shipley* (2014).

While very effort has been made to obtain permission for images used here, some, as usual, remain elusive or unresponsive. Any transgressions will be put right in future printings, where informed.

Paul Chrystal, summer 2023
www.paulchrystal.com

# Bradford Pubs

The **Upper Globe** was at 14 Toller Lane, closing in 2001, a victim of the Bradford riots. *M. G. Spiller 25 June 2006*

The **Theatre Tavern** was on Manningham Lane. It was delisted as a grade-II listed building in 1997, having been demolished in 1989 to make way for the obligatory car park and inner ring road scheme.

This curious name of the **Second West Hotel** reflects the wild west theme that was characteristic of this pub at 314 Cemetery Road. Lidget Green derives from a farm in the adjoining village of Clayton, which was called Lidget, a name which means loud or roaring water, or the gateway to the people's well. Sadly little that is green remains.

The **Royal Engineer** was a favourite watering hole for mill workers nearby and those at Bowling Iron Works. Bowling Iron Works was founded in 1788; Terry's Mill opened in 1823, and Albion Mill, and Perseverance Mill after 1850. Industry Mill was destroyed in a fire in 1890 but rebuilt in brick. In 1935 Jubilee Mills opened. Greenfield greyhound stadium was nearby too and no doubt the hotel benefitted from celebrating winners. James William Griffith Watkins published this card; he was a local crane driver and photographer. The pub was demolished in 1962. Joseph Stocks of Shibden Head provided the beer here – just one of their 111 licensed premises.

Continuing the military theme the **Artillery Arms** was on Bowling Back Lane; the **Gunner Inn** in North Street; the **Wellington Inn** was at Low Moor, from 1895. Not to be outdone (the Napoleon was at 343 Wakefield Road; originally known as **The Central**, the Napoleon opened in 1856 and was a Hammonds United Breweries house in 1889, sold in 1959. The building is Grade II Listed. The industrial nature of the place is reflected in the **Furnace** also once on Bowling Back Lane; the **Hand & Shuttle** at 50 Tong Street from 1822 while the **Moulders Arms** was situated on Sticker Lane, also from 1822. **The Yarnspinners Arms** was in Burrow Road; the **Patent Hammer Inn** from 1872 and **Corn Mill Inn** were at Wibsey (1886). Days off from work were catered for by the **Live & Let Live** in Thornton (1885) and the **Old Arm Chair Inn**, Bolton Road (1886). **The Gallopers** was on Busfield Road, built in the 1970s and designed on a fairground ride theme. It has lain empty and boarded up since 2015.

Dudley Hill had the benefit of being at the junction of three turnpikes: the Cutler Heights to Bradford turnpike (1740) down Rooley Lane; the Bradford to Wakefield turnpike (1752) and the Dudley Hill, Killinghall and Harrogate turnpike (1804) along Sticker Lane. It enjoys an important role in trolleybus history when in 1911 Britain's first trolleybus service started between Laisterdyke and Dudley Hill. The service ended in 1972, making it also the last trolleybus service in the UK. The only listed building in Dudley Hill is the Grade II listed former Dudley Hill Picture Palace.

The **Airdale** at 2 Otley Road, Shipley; it's modern namesake in Bradford, the **Airedale**, is at 77 Otley Road, it was a Royal Antediluvian Order of Buffaloes (RAOB) club. The Shipley pub was demolished for road widening and redevelopment.

Paul Jennings has done some detailed research on the Airedale Inn, as published in his *The Local: A History of the English Pub* (2011) ; here is some of what he has found:

> A licence was granted to Thomas Peel for the newly-built Airedale Inn in 1848, chiefly because of its stabling, according to the magistrates…

The photograph shown here was taken in 1910, the year that Francis Catterick and his wife Sarah had taken the pub. The posters on the wall between them advertise that members' tickets were now available for the Bradford Amateur FC, season 1910-11, and that the forthcoming final of the Priestley Cup would take place at Park Avenue between Great Horton and Undercliffe, which the latter went on to win by 118 runs. The Cattericks were to remain at the Airedale until the summer of 1921…Under the Cattericks it had been a free house, selling both Tetley and Hammonds beers, but eventually became a Tetley's house. It was this brewery which built a new Airedale as part of the clearance and redevelopment of the area in the late 1950s and early 1960s.

Other pubs on the Otley Road included the **Olive Branch**, the **George**, **New Inn** and **Cambridge Hotel**.

The **Boar's Head** is seen here to the left of the Hey's Gold Cup sign at Market Street. The pub was up and running by 1822, when the publican was George Pollard; it was demolished to make way for road widening. The pub's name is not without significance – boars can be seen all over the city and a giant gilded version looks down from the top of the **Old Crown** in Ivegate. It features on the city crest and therefore on the badge of Bradford Park Avenue FC; there is one on a black drainpipe running down the side of City Hall. It probably all started with the forests and the boars which roamed in them which covered the site of the city in the Middle Ages.

There is, of course, another **Boar's Head** still very much alive in Queensbury and there was a **Wild Boar** in Spinkwell Terrace from 1872.

The **Spring Row Tavern** was situated at 4 Spring Row on White Abbey Road. This pub was notorious for the bare knuckle fighting and boxing held on the premises. The photo shows licensee Harry Hanson with his wife and children in about 1910. The sign on the wall would suggest that Harry was a Bradford City supporter.

The **Fox and Hounds**, at 1 Commercial Street, lent its name to its location which became known as Fox Corner; it was originally a Melbourne Ales of Leeds pub but became a Tetley's house when Melbourne was taken over. The pub was demolished in the early 70s for road widening.

The **Branch** was at 105 Bradford Road and Otley road corner; it was formerly a coaching inn called, appropriately enough, the **Coach and Horses**. The Prince's Hall is behind, to the left of the pub, and was used as a cinema. The pub closed in 2016 to be demolished two years later.

The **Angel** is at 9 Northgate, Baildon, and can be identified here (just) by the Tetley's sign above the bus on the left; both buses are West Yorkshire Road Car buses. This is the oldest pub in Baildon close to the **Malt Shovel**, a fellow Green King pub. The pub name reflects the ancient connection between religious establishments and hostels for travellers, mainly monks moving between monasteries.

Baildon has an important place in British Gypsy community history. A 1929 report states that annual Gypsy Parties had taken place two to three hundred years before to 1770 when it was reported to be an established ancient custom. In 1881, up to 5,000 people are said to have paid to get in. Over time the event was taken over by local residents, who dressed up as Gypsies and formed 'tribes', proceeds going to the local Horticultural Society. After 1897 the tradition died out, because the 'real Gypsies' were nowhere to be seen. However, in 1929 the event was revived to raise funds for Baildon Hospital. A local resident, John Keen, then contacted the King of the Gypsies, Xavier Petulengro, and they re-established large Gypsy Parties at Baildon, recorded on Pathe News films shown nationally in cinemas. The Gypsy Parties ended with the start of the Second World War, never to return.

The **Fox & Pheasant** was at 748 Little Horton Lane from 1822. It was rebuilt but closed in 2006.

The **Roebuck Inn** was on the corner of Clifford Street and Nelson Street. It has now been demolished to make way for some wasteland masquerading as a car park. There was also a **Roebuck** at 921 Harrogate Road in Greengates, similarly demolished in deference to a frozen food supermarket, and another in Utley, near Keighley. In Baildon there was a **Roebuck Inn** between **The Angel** and **The Malt Shovel** and to the right of Lynton House. The Inn closed in 1927. Roebucks are clearly an endangered species in this part of the world.

Opened in the 1750s in Tyrrel Street the **New Inn** hosted Bradford's first flower show in 1827. Not only that, the pub had its own pig market in the stable yard. The postcard shows a rebuild after the old New Inn was demolished to accommodate the Manchester Road in the 1960s. The towers of the New Victoria cinema loom in the background.

**Dick Hudson's** was originally on the old packhorse route between Bingley and Ilkley and was an old farmhouse-cum-inn called **The Plough Boy**. When Eldwick Road was closed, the business located to its present site, Highgate Farm, and was named the **Fleece Inn**. Thomas Hudson took over the inn in 1809, but it was during the tenure of his son, Dick Hudson between 1850 and 1878 that the pub really took off.

# Cinemas and Theatres

Bradford was, in the golden age of the cinema, awash with picture houses – as befits the city that is home to the peerless National Science and Media Museum.

Work began in 1914 to build the Regent theatre-cinema on Manningham Lane between Fountain Street and Drewton Street; the façade facing onto Manningham Lane was described as "a handsome elevation in the French Classic style" with white terracotta and a central section with four part-fluted decorated pillars supporting a Greek Ionic capital and architrave and central cyma with the whole topped by an octagonal tower and similarly octagon-faced dome with flagpole.

William Frederick George Phillips (1870-1940) was a master photographer with a business in Bradford providing a film hire and transport service to picture houses springing up across the city. His Imperial Animated Film Company had premises in Thorpe Chambers, Hustlergate. Phillips had this business opportunity after Cecil Wray's Film Service of Eccleshill moved to Leeds.

Will Phillips was also managing director and prime mover of the company behind the new Regent project. September 1913 saw the new company registered as Regent Picture House (Bradford) Ltd with £20,000 in £1 shares. Seating capacity was 1377, upholstered in dark blue velvet and matching Wilton carpet to contrast with the decorations of white and gold.

The Regent was equipped from the start with a stage 35 feet wide and 30 feet deep, two dressing rooms and orchestra pit. The rectangular proscenium with an opening 30 feet wide was topped by imposing plaster figures in a 'coat of arms' style design.

In 1947 the Regent was taken over by Sol Sheckman's Essoldo Circuit based in Newcastle-upon-Tyne and the cinema renamed as Essoldo; a huge vertical illuminated fin-like name sign was added above the canopy that was totally out of character with the rest of the building. 'By this time it was looking rather seedy and neglected with an auditorium smelling of Jeyes Fluid sprayed regularly "For Your Comfort" said the screen advert. At some point the octagonal tower, dome and flagpole had been removed'. (https://www.bradfordtimeline.co.uk/regent.htm) The Essoldo closed on Saturday 30th October 1965.

In 1968 it reopened as an Asian cinema run by the Pakistan National Film Club and Munir Ahmed Khan.

The Essoldo Circuit was a family concern; the curious name Essoldo is made up from the first names of Esther (his wife), Soloman and Dorothy (his daughter).

*Much of the above comes from Cinema History Researched & Compiled by the late Colin Sutton Copyright © 1980/2006, Colin Sutton; the entries following also owe a huge debt to Colin Sutton's extensive and meticulous research.*

The Savoy was in bustling Darley Street opposite Kirkgate Market and the Central Library. When it was built in 1920, it was the largest city centre cinema with a seating capacity of 1,593 in its stalls, circle and gallery. The *Bradford Daily Argus* was most impressed with its pillar-free views:

> Inside, the arrangements for seating are on the most modern and up-to-date principles. The area gives ample opportunity for a centre view of the picture and the seats in the side galleries are angled towards the screen so that one does not need to screw oneself sideways.

Non-smokers too would have been impressed by the ventilation system:

> the plant also had exhaust ventilation to remove vitiated air and smoke continuously, with a capacity of almost 2,000 cubic feet of fresh air per hour which was equivalent to completely changing the air of the theatre once in every five minutes.

Disaster struck on the evening of Saturday 18th January 1936 just before 10pm when the film jammed in the projector and caught fire. Even though an asbestos blanket was thrown over the projector, it blew up hurling the two projectionists, John H. Hewitt and John Lavelle, out of the operating room and down a flight of stone stairs leading to the rewind room. The third operator, John Scott, was in the rewind room under the projection room and was blown out of the small room by the explosion. We learn from Chris Sutton (https://www.bradfordtimeline.co.uk/savoy.htm) that:

> The projection room at the rear of the stalls had one of its side walls separating the operating room from the pit area completely blown out and huge chunks of plaster and concrete were flung into the theatre. Several patrons suffered cuts, burns and shock. Several seats were damaged. The manager, Robert Burns, said "there was no panic and the place was cleared in a few minutes". Around 1,500 people were in the auditorium at the time.
> 
> Due to closure, the film programme was transferred to the Regent in Manningham Lane – on lease to ABC at the time.

The Savoy re-opened on 3rd February 1936 with *Anna Karenina* – starring Greta Garbo. Seating capacity was now 662 in the stalls arranged in three blocks with two aisles; circle 489 and gallery 374 also in three blocks. The total was 1,525 which later reduced to 1,517. In 1939 ABC closed the Savoy with the final performance on Saturday 15th April 1939.

The impressive four storey stone Alexandra Hotel with its imposing columned entrance has a leading role in the founding of The Empire, for it was on the large lawn at the rear of the hotel that architect W.J Sprague designed the Empire Music Hall which opened on the 30th January 1899 with music hall acts, notably Stan Laurel in 1906, a young Charlie Chaplin (in 1906, 1909 and 1910) and W.C Fields (1911).

From 1914 Francis Laidler's newly-built Alhambra Theatre, just a few yards away across the road, caused major problems for the Empire as audiences declined, resulting in its closure as a variety theatre in April 1916. Laidler later that year reopened the Empire and called it the Empire Theatre & Opera House with a season of plays; this lasted only about fifteen months as the stage was completely destroyed by fire in 1917. It reopened as the Empire Cinema on 11th February 1918.

Colin Sutton reveals *'that its impressive and atmospheric pillared foyer led to an auditorium of some 1381 seats in typical old variety theatre style with a horseshoe circle and a steep stepped gallery and pillared side boxes'*.

In 1923 the name changed to Empire Super Cinema and in 1926 it came under the control of Harry Buxton's Empire (Bradford) Ltd who wanted to rebuild the stage and present Cine-Variety which had become popular in other halls. This did not happen due to objections from Francis Laidler of the nearby Alhambra Theatre, determined as he was to eradicate any competition.

On the evening of 25th January 1952 a fire broke out which damaged the gallery and ceiling and broke through the roof. A notice appeared the following day . . ."The Management regret that owing to unforeseen circumstances the cinema will be closed for a few days."

In fact it was rather optimistic as this was the final curtain and the cinema never did reopen.

The Ritz opened on 8th May 1939 in a prime city centre location at the junction of Broadway and Leeds Road. It was part of John Maxwell's flourishing ABC (Associated British Cinemas) circuit, as were Bradford's Regent and Savoy. Maxwell (1876-1940) had a controlling interest in the Pathé distribution company and established Elstree Studios. The Savoy closed in April 1939 and the licence was transferred to the new Ritz.

On the extreme outer side of the foyer circle staircases were huge pillars to accentuate the grandeur of the entrance foyer. Large pendant light fittings dominated the high ceiling. The staircases and inner lobbies were thickly carpeted and the entrance foyer floor rubber tiled. Decoration was in warm and welcoming tints… the auditorium was splendidly proportioned and a true classic of William Riddell Glen [the architect] design with 2,037 seats in a sumptuous visual setting.

The Ardent deaf aid system was fitted – a first in a Bradford cinema.

The Ritz escaped wartime bombing but the flooding Bradford Beck wreaked havoc here. Initially The Ritz did not screen X-certificate adult-only films but in 1952, as a result of a circuit decision, the policy was reversed and showed such X-films as (in screening order) . . .

*A Streetcar Named Desire* (Warner 1951, brutal rape).
*The Big Heat* (Columbia 1953, screen violence – coffee in the face).
*House of Wax* in 3-D (Warner 1953, fire horror).
*Riot in Cell Block Eleven* (United Artists 1954, prison violence).
*Rebel Without a Cause* (Warner 1955 CinemaScope, juvenile violence).
*Rififi* (Pathé 1955, robbery and bloodshed).

In 1969 EMI took control of ABPC (Associated British Picture Corporation); the Ritz continued to be known simply as the ABC. The ABC closed on 3rd August 1974; the building was demolished in March 1988.

The New Victoria was built on Brewery Street on the site of the old William Whittaker's Brewery which had stopped brewing and malting in 1928. This magnificent red brick theatre also offered a cinema, ballroom, restaurant and tea room/café and cost £250,000.

> It is claimed to have used some two million bricks and a thousand tons of steel …and is a fine example of Flemish Bond brickwork with supports in white terracotta. The Italian Renaissance design of its interior adapted to modern (1930) requirements and sumptuous furnishings were to be marvelled at for the next four decades.
> 
> *https://www.bradfordtimeline.co.uk/newvic.htm*

Bradford architect William Illingworth made good use of his studies of the designs of Filippo Brunelleschi (1377-1446) a leading light in the Italian Renaissance with his revival of classical forms of architecture based on mathematical, proportion and an understanding of perspective and the construction of octagonal domes as in the Duomo in Florence. The website goes on to tell us:

> The theatre auditorium designed for 3,500 seats was acoustically perfect for stage and classical orchestral performances. The fact that the circle and balcony were set back from the stalls with minimal overhang meant that every seat provided a perfect uninterrupted view of the stage and orchestra pit; but uniquely a splendid view of the richly decorated auditorium walls, ceiling and dome.

Illingworth thought it important that patrons always be aware and enjoy the spectacular and sumptuous surroundings whatever price paid for the seat.

During the evening of 31st August 1940, the Luftwaffe bombed Bradford; the nearby Odeon was badly damaged but in the New Victoria Ballroom dancing was well under way when the bombs started dropping; the band stopped playing only momentarily then continued while the raid was in progress. There was no war damage to the building. The Gaumont Ballroom, as it was now known, finally closed on Saturday 30th December 1961.

In the '50s and '60s the Gaumont was the largest indoor concert venue in the north of England; its excellent acoustics attracted big names and included Bill Haley and the Comets (17th February 1957), Count Basie, Paul Anka, Helen Shapiro, Frankie Lane (19th October 1953), Buddy Holly (9th March 1958) and Tom Jones (1968). Not forgetting, of course, the Beatles – followed later by the Rolling Stones (19th October 1963 and 4th October 1965).

The Beatles first played the Gaumont on 2nd February 1963 as a 'bottom of the bill' support act to 16-year old Helen Shapiro. They came back on 21st December 1963 headlining two sell-out performances supported by the Barron-Knights, The Fourmost, Billy J. Kramer and the Dakotas, and Cilla Black. In 1964 they returned again on 9th October when John Lennon celebrated his 24th birthday by autographing the dressing room wall with "John Lennon was here 9 Octbr 1964" [*sic*]. The group were paid £850 for the two sets.
1968 saw the closure of the Gaumont.

It was the demolition of the former Central Mills Wool Combing owned by Joseph Cooper Jnr. & Co Ltd that allowed a large site on Manchester Road next to the Oddfellows Arms near the junction with Hope Street and opposite the defunct Palace Theatre to be developed for one of Oscar Deutsch's Odeons in 1938. At the time Bradford enjoyed an embarrassment of riches: the Alhambra Theatre and the awe-inspiring New Victoria Theatre/Cinema, ballroom and restaurant complex with its 3,318 seats – so Deutsch would have to come up with something good if the Odeon was to compete.

He did:

The exterior was brilliantly illuminated with the lit chandeliers of the circle foyer/lounge sparkling through the huge windows together with lights all the way up the continuous vertical glass window of the tower. The all-glass top of the tower was radiant in red/green coloured neon lighting making it a landmark visible across the city.

(*https://www.bradfordtimeline.co.uk/odeon.htm*

When it opened the Bradford Odeon was the largest in the chain with 2,713 seats (1,750 stalls and 963 circle) – flagship Odeon Leicester Square had only 2,116 seats at its opening. Colin Sutton gives us the detail of the destructive bombing raid of Saturday August 31st 1940:

Ten minutes after the cinema had cleared, the bombs dropped crashing through the roof into the front stalls and causing fires instantly. As the ceiling came down heavy metal chandeliers crashed onto the seats. The stage fittings, screen, footlights, orchestra pit and front stalls seats were destroyed. The landmark glass tower and the entrance frontage were also damaged.

The Odeon Theatre closed on Saturday 22nd March 1969. Confusingly, the name 'Odeon' was transferred to the new converted 'twins' (The Gaumont), as announced in the release from Odeon: "*Watch for opening date of Bradford's Twin luxury Theatres (formerly the Gaumont)*".

The name 'Odeon' is often believed to be an acronym for "Oscar Deutsch Entertains (or Entertaining) Our Nation" – not a bit of it ! It derives from the Greek Ὠιδεῖον, 'Oideion', a singing place, as in the famous Odeon of Pericles in Athens at the south eastern foot of the Acropolis, next to the entrance to the Theatre of Dionysus. It had already been used as a theatre name and for cinemas in France and Italy in the 1920s, for example as in L'Odeon in Paris which suggested a luxury or even a classical touch. Apparently, a friend of Oscar Deutsch had also seen the name Odeon in Tunis and recommended it particularly as it started with 'OD' the initials of Oscar Deutsch. The name "Nickelodeon" was coined in 1888 and was widely used to describe small cinemas in the United States from 1905.

The Picture House (sometimes called the Town Hall Square Picture House) could be found at 4 Thornton Road; in 1912 its first proprietor, John Goodman, converted the stone-built four-storey former warehouse into a two-deck cinema together with café. A large basement area was used a billiard hall. The upper floors were leased out to commercial businesses with a clothing factory on the top floor. Colin Sutton says:

> The elaborate new frontage at street level with its mahogany and glass doors opened into a miniature court with its marble and mahogany base and richly embellished staircases leading to the first floor café. Here refreshments were available to off-street customers and to cinema patrons particularly of its luxurious balcony… from the café to the balcony there were thick Turkish carpets *"to deaden the sound of a footfall and Ionic pillars and furnishings in the Adams style"*.
>
> *https://www.bradfordtimeline.co.uk/tatler.htm*

In 1918 the Picture House played host to Bradford Theosophical Society for special public meetings featuring a national lecturer of some standing. On Sunday afternoons from 7th to 28th April and for nine weeks throughout November and December 1918 crowds of up to 700 assembled to hear Miss Clara Margaret Codd (1876-1971), a suffragette and theosophist, whose talks covered Reincarnation, The Hope of the World, The Other side of Death and The Power of Thought. *". . . the Picture House was often filled with audiences thrilled by the inspired messages delivered."*

In 1931 the cinema was bought by Regal Cinemas (Warrington) Ltd with Leeds-born Harry Buxton in charge. He changed the name to Tatler Picture House; from 1935 it was the New Tatler. On the evening of 12th December 1945 and only 10 minutes after the last performance had finished at 9.25pm, a fire devastated the building. Then, on 29th September 1946 heavy storms caused the Bradford Beck, which runs under Thornton Road outside the New Tatler building, to burst and the waters poured through the former cinema. The site was demolished in the 1960s as part of the

A fascinating and quite unique structure, the Prince's Theatre was built at the same time as and on top of the Star Music Hall (later the Palace Theatre) as the only double-stacked theatre in the country. The Prince's Theatre was named after the Prince Of Wales who was later to become King Edward VII. The auditorium and stage were on top of and directly in line with the Star Music Hall/ Palace Theatre below – the latter being partly underground but due to the slope of the land the Prince's Theatre was above ground with its own entrance and exit on the higher St John's Street near the bottom of Little Horton Lane. The street name comes from the short-lived, never consecrated St John's Church which previously occupied the site.

The inside of the Prince's interior was much flashier than the humble Star. With raked stalls, stepped dress circle and steep-stepped gallery both of horseshoe shape it originally accommodated an astonishing 2,880 people both seated and standing. It offered 13 dressing rooms, a spacious green room and ample storage rooms. The gallery had 16 rows of backless wooden benches and six rows in each side gallery. There were wooden benches also in the pit along with a wide promenade area at the sides and rear.

11.30pm on the evening of Tuesday 16th July 1878 saw a disastrous fire break out and spread rapidly causing the roof to fall in. By 12.30pm most of the theatres had been destroyed.

Colin Sutton takes up the story:

The origin of the fire was a mystery. That week a play *Simon, or More Ways than One* was being performed by James Taylor's visiting company who lost all of their costumes in the blaze. By coincidence both the Prince's and the Star Music Hall had been rented by William Morgan who had recently gone into liquidation. Only the day before, Charlie Rice, lessee of the Theatre Royal in Manningham Lane had just signed to take the lease of the Prince's for ten years and had plans to improve it. Although Rice had not yet taken control, it was his own staff from the Theatre Royal (then closed for alterations) who were working backstage as the Prince's regular crew were on strike.
https://www.bradfordtimeline.co.uk/theatres/prince.htm

The rebuilt Prince's Theatre reopened on Christmas Eve 1879 with a performance of *Golden Locks*. In July 1896 Walter Reynolds of the Theatre Royal in Leeds bought both the Prince's and the Palace Theatre; on 8th September 1902 he leased the Prince's Theatre to Walter J Piper, his son-in-law, and one Francis Laidler, then a newcomer to theatre.

Six months later Piper died and Laidler carried on as sole lessee: he soon brought London touring productions to Bradford and started his run of spectacular pantomimes. It remained a theatre with touring shows and pantomimes until 1935 when Laidler permanently transferred the now famous pantomimes to his newer and better-equipped Alhambra Theatre across the road. Closure came in June 1960.

The Star Music hall changed name several times over its existance being known as the Peoples' Palace, the Palace Theatre and Concert Hall Court (St John's Court)

Seating in the pit was in two blocks with centre and side aisles accommodating 1,100 persons seated and standing at rear. The steep stepped gallery had six rows of 400 seats plus 600 standing giving 2,100 in total. There were six private boxes, three at each side and the walls either side of the stage splayed to allow better viewing from the side gallery end seats. Both pit and gallery each had a refreshment room/bar at the rear of their promenades.

The Peoples' Palace, as it was now called, has a particular place in the history of cinema in Bradford for it was here that on Easter Monday 6th April 1896 that Lumière's Cinématographe of projected moving images was demonstrated for the first time in the area. Advertising for the event went as follows:

Peoples' Palace, Bradford. A wonderful attraction has been engaged for the Easter week programme Monday, 6th April 1896. It consists of the most wonderful invention of the the age – The Cinématographe – now packing the London Halls at every performance. Once nightly. 6d to 10/-d.

The Palace closed on Saturday 28th May 1938 with "Paulo – the singing clown and BBC Palace of Varieties sensation" top of the bill.

The magnificent Alhambra Theatre is named after the Alhambra palace in Granada, Spain, the residence of the Emir of the Emirate of Granada; the name Alhambra derives from the Arabic ٱلْقَلْعَةُ ٱلْحَمْرَاءُ Al-Qa'lat Al-Hamra' meaning the fortress that is reddish-brown.

It was built in 1913 on the site of the 'Morley Street Waste' at a cost of £20,000 for theatre impresario Francis Laidler, and opened on 18th March 1914. Today the main house seats 1,456. Originally the only advance ticket sales were for the boxes, hence the name 'Box Office'. The 'Retained Foyer' is the only remaining part of the original theatre's entrance. The Stalls once had no formal seating – only benches and chairs at the front. The Dress Circle contains what were, at the time, the best seats in the house and is so called because you were expected to dress up. The Upper Circle is known as The Gods because of the plaster Gods holding up the ceiling.

Formerly – The Royal Alexandra Theatre; The Theatre Royal Picture House; The Irving Royal Cinema; Classic Royal Cinema. This Theatre Royal shares its name with The Theatre Royal on Duke Street with which it is sometimes confused. The Manningham Lane theatre opened as the Alexandra Theatre on 26th December 1864 with the pantomime *All That Glitters is not Gold*. The building cost £6,000, and could seat around 1,800 people, 200 in the Dress Boxes, 250 in the Upper Boxes, 600 in the Pit, and 750 in the Gallery.

Unfortunately perhaps, the theatre is best known for being the last place where Henry Irving performed before his death in October 1905 at the Midland Hotel in Bradford after a performance of 'Becket' at the Theatre. The Theatre Royal had films in its repertoire from the late 1890s; in 1921 it was closed as a live theatre and the auditorium was converted into a full time cinema. The Cinema opened as the Theatre Royal Picture House on 5th of December 1921 with a showing of the Charlie Chaplin film *The Idle Class*.

In 1965 the cinema's owners went bankrupt; it was bought and refurbished by Expo 20 Ltd. who reopened it as the Irving Royal Cinema, as a tribute to Henry Irving and opened on 27th of February 1967 with the Al Jolson film *The Singing Fool*. In October the same year however, Classic Cinemas took over the building and renamed it the Classic Royal Cinema, ignominiously dropping the Irving name.

The Classic closed on 16th of November 1974 after a showing of *The Graduate*.

The Duke Street Theatre Royal was a wooden building which first opened as the Liver Theatre in 1841. The Theatre was later rebuilt by Charles Rice and renamed the Theatre Royal when it reopened on August 13th, 1844. On 25th June 1887 The ERA carried a report on the 'Early Drama of Bradford', and in it they wrote about the Duke Street Theatre Royal:

'Another theatre dear to the memory of many an old Bradford playgoer was the old Theatre Royal, Duke-street, or the old "wooden box," as it was often called. As the home for so many years of what was styled the " legitimate drama " it certainly was a shabby concern. It was erected in the year 1841 as a theatre for Mrs Wild, and went by the name of the "Liver" theatre'.

*I am indebted to "Matthew Lloyd, http://www.arthurlloyd.co.uk for much of the above material on The Theatre Royal.*

St. George's Hall, built in 1886 as Bradford's General Post Office this magnificent grade II listed building sports a polished granite frontage and is in the Northern Renaissance architectural style: an architectural highlight in the Little Germany area of the city.

In 2000, St Peter's House received a glass extension linking it to the beautiful gardens of Bradford Cathedral, a calm oasis in the centre of town and a fine example of modern intervention in an historic area.

In November 2011, Kala Sangam completed the Ganges Hall

refurbishment, which – with air-conditioning, multi-stage lighting and sound systems, a fully sprung dance floor and superior redecoration – made it one of the finest performance venues in Bradford. The Kala Sangam Arts Centre was launched in March 2012.

Kala Sangam was founded in 1993 by Dr Shripati Upadhyaya, a consultant clinical psychologist with a special interest in the creative use of arts to help people with disabilities. His dream was to establish a unique organisation that delivered high quality south Asian arts through innovative collaborations and that would be accessible to people of all ages and abilities. Working alongside his wife, Dr Geetha Upadhyaya, a consultant in Metabolic Medicine and trained Bharatanatyam dancer, Dr Shripati first set up Kala Sangam in Leeds, in 1993. In 1996, the company moved to the Carlisle Business Centre in Bradford, while they looked for a permanent home in Bradford to grow the company.

St George's Hall was designed with a seating capacity of 3,500; the hall now seats up to 1,350 people and 1,550 for standing concerts. It is the oldest concert hall still in use in the United Kingdom and the third oldest in the whole of Europe. German Jewish wool merchants attracted to Bradford because of its textile industry financed the building. Built of ashlar sandstone masonry in neoclassical style, the building was opened on 29th August 1853 by Queen Victoria and Prince Albert.

The venue was seen as a well-meaning solution to the erratic moral compass of the working classes, to deflect them

from their predilection for rowdy pubs and the brothels attached to them.

The photos, courtesy of *Bradford Telegraph & Argus*, show the Hall in 1953 and the audience at a school choir concert at St George's Hall in December, 1967. St George's Hall is the third-oldest concert hall in Europe., Charles Dickens took to the stage to give his first-ever public reading of *Bleak House*. Half a century later, '*For Positively One Week Only from Monday, February 13, 1905*', Harry Houdini transfixed the audience.

# Parks

Manningham or Lister Park was laid out in 1870 centred around Manningham Hall and its grounds, its grand entrance is seen above. The hall had been bought by Bradford Corporation at "half real value" from Samuel Cunliffe Lister, the man who built Lister's Mill, on condition it be used as a public park as seen below. Once a deer park, Lister Park contains six listed buildings. In 1898 Lister was disturbed to find the hall in a dilapidated state. He gifted the proceeds from the previous sale to the Corporation to replace the hall with a permanent memorial to Edmund Cartwright – the inventor of the power loom upon which much of Bradford's prosperity had been founded. Cartwright Hall was completed in time for the Bradford Exhibition of 1904.

The botanical gardens are a thing of beauty; there is also a geological trail winding throughout the various beds, which are landscaped around the stream which is a re-creation of Thornton Force.

A botanical garden or botanic garden is not just any old garden; it is a garden dedicated to the collection, cultivation, preservation and display of a wide range of plants labelled with their botanical names. It may contain specialist plant collections such as cacti and other succulent plants, herb gardens, plants from particular parts of the world, and so on. Botanical gardens are often run by universities or other scientific research organisations, and have associated herbaria and research programmes in plant taxonomy or some other aspect of botanical science. Their role is to maintain documented collections of living plants for the purposes of scientific research, conservation, display, and education. The origin of modern botanical gardens is generally traced to the appointment of professors of botany to the medical faculties of universities in 16th century Renaissance Italy, which also entailed the curation of a medicinal garden.

The first of their kind in Northern England, the Mughal Water Gardens are a fusion of Islamic and Indian architectural styles, combining terraces and paths, grassed areas and avenues of trees divided by water channels, cascades and pools in a traditional rectangular design. It reflects the cultural heritage of the area's large British Asian community. A quarter of a million litres of water is pumped through underground pipes and perpetually recycled to create an effect reminiscent of a sloping Indian hillside.

The Mughal dynasty was founded by the Emperor Babur in 1527, lasting until 1857. During that time it produced a number of visionary and charismatic kings whose contribution to art, architecture and horticulture was peerless. Mughal architecture is a synthesis between Islamic and Hindu architectural styles prevalent in the Indian sub-continent.

The open air Lido was constructed in 1915. Despite its popularity in its early years, by the 1930s interest had begun to wane, not least because it no longer met the standards of hygiene the public expected. The council carried out a modernisation scheme in 1937 which involved the installation of a filtration, sterilisation and heating plant. A cafe came too. By 1982 extensive repairs were required. The Lido closed in 1983 and was demolished in 1991.

Peel Park was Bradford's first public park; it is named after Sir Robert Peel (1788-1850). Its origins stem from a public meeting which took place in St George's Hall in August 1850 to discuss the creation of a park as a memorial to Sir Robert Peel who had died that year. A government donation of £1,500 was complemented by donations from Sir Titus Salt among others to purchase 64 acres of land that was subsequently named Peel Park Estate; 56 acres of this land was developed as Peel Park. The park was opened in 1853 and a series of galas were held there to raise funds to pay off the remaining debt for the purchase of the land and its layout as a park—this took 12 years.

The Peel statue was Bradford's first public statue and was originally located in what was Peel Place on Leeds Road, but re-erected after 1926 in Peel Park after Kassapian's Warehouse on Leeds Road was demolished. Peel is kept company by a life-size statue of two Roman matronae, one representing Autumn (1869) and one representing Spring (1877) – both donated by the Bradford Band of Hope Union. All three statues are grade II listed.

There are at least 15 other statues of Robert Peel, one of which is in Bradford's Wool Exchange; all but one, which is in Tasmania, are in the UK. He is also honoured by fifteen pubs, including one in Heckmondwike.

The Conservatory – Orchid House – in Peel Park, around 1915.

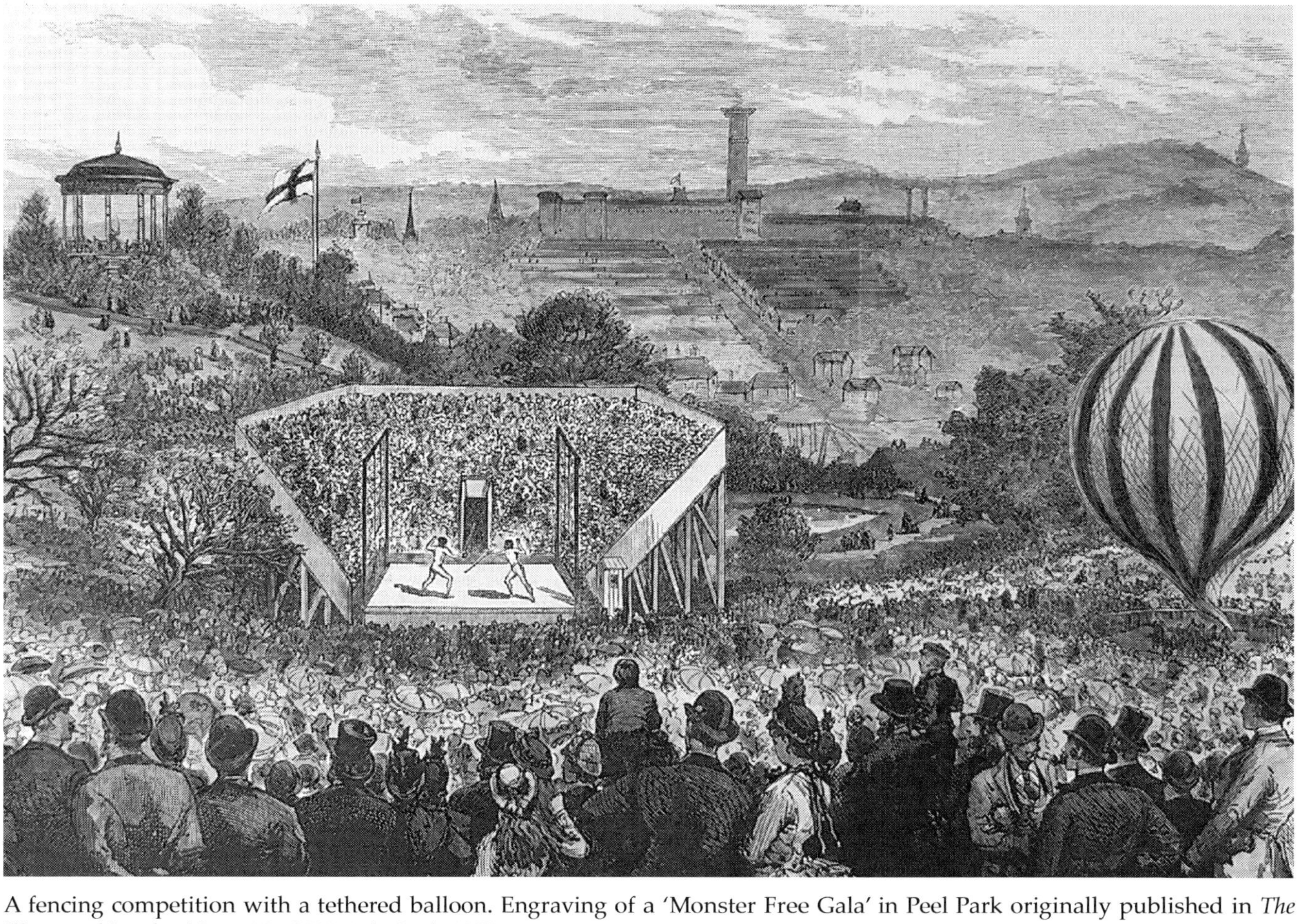

A fencing competition with a tethered balloon. Engraving of a 'Monster Free Gala' in Peel Park originally published in *The Illustrated London News*, No 2515, July 2nd, 1887.

# Bradford Buildings

Part built in New Street (later Market Street) by private subscription in 1782; the Old Piece Hall, or Market Hall was completed by Benjamin Rawson, lord of the manor, who brought the idea back from his travels in Italy. No one really liked it so there was much joy when it was demolished in 1825 to make way for the Exchange Building.

Today, Piece Hall Yard is a pedestrianised street just off Hustlergate. The Piece Hall is long gone, but the yard keeps alive Bradford's heritage and the city's historical association with the textiles trade. A piece hall is where the trading of "pieces" of cloth was conducted.

Piece Hall Yard is home to the entrance to the Bradford Club, a traditional gentleman's club, and also the Peace Museum which displays exhibits relating to peace and conflict resolution throughout the world. The museum is the only museum dedicated to the history and stories of peace, peacemakers and peace movements in the UK.

The idea came from Gerald Drewett of the Give Peace a Chance Trust, and, in 1990 this was given impetus when Shireen Shah, an MA student at Bradford University's Peace Studies Department, completed a dissertation proposing a 'Museum for Peace'. Two years on, the International Network of Museums for Peace held its first conference at the University of Bradford in 1992, during which it was proposed that a Peace Museum be established in Bradford. Initially called 'The National Peace Museum Project', the Museum was established in 1994 through a five-year grant from the Joseph Rowntree Charitable Foundation and operated from the Wool Exchange. In 1998 the Museum moved to the top floor of 10 Piece Hall Yard, in Bradford city centre.

The Top o' t' Town Chapel, Westgate is described in *The Baptists of Yorkshire* by Rev. J. Brown Morgan and Rev. C.E. Shipley that

> The private room in which worship was conducted soon became too "strait" for the members attending, and "*a place of dissoluteness*" known as "*The Cockpit*" was transformed into a sanctuary. It is recorded that the Church was too poor to seat the new sanctuary, so they carried the stools on which they sat with them to the house of God. In 1755, the first place of worship was built in Westgate, which was then regarded as "*the top of the town*." The new sanctuary became known as "the top of the town chapel.

This building was superseded by the Westgate Chapel in Carlisle Road.

The Independents had a chapel in Horton Lane from 1782; in 1811 Kirkgate Wesleyan Chapel was built; in 1823 the Sion Baptist Chapel was erected in Bridge Street; and in 1825 East Brook Chapel was opened.

This replaced the butter market which was on the ground floor of the Toll Booth in Ivegate as part of the Green Market – a much-loved building of 1824. However, 1824 saw a complete revamp of market facilities in Bradford with this being built behind the Manor Hall. Kirkgate Market replaced it in 1866 after its demolition. Against much popular disapproval the Green Market building was demolished to make way for the Kirkgate Shopping Centre which opened in 1976. The 1845 *Ibbetson's Directory of the Borough of Bradford* lists fourteen butter factors working out of the butter market.

Bradford Children's Hospital in St Mary's Road, Manningham was founded in 1883. It closed in 1988 when services were transferred to St Luke's with part of the building continuing as the Nightingale Nursing Home.

How did it start? The story of Bradford Children's Hospital begins in 1862 when some women of the All Saints' Sisterhood – a high Anglican guild in London – following their vocation of visiting the poor in the parish of St Jude's – went into the poorest parts of Bradford, then known as Black Abbey. Unsurprisingly, they found there many sick and ailing children who would clearly benefit from being cared for in cleaner, more sanitary surroundings where they could be properly fed and nurtured.

So, in the summer of 1863 the sisters converted two houses in Hanover Square into a small hospital with a dozen beds and did the nursing themselves, with the help of funds obtained mainly from personal friends. Their good work soon started to draw attention and in 1884 a meeting was held at the Town Hall at which a committee was appointed to take over the management of the hospital. The committee was non-sectarian but the "sisters" continued to do all the work in the hospital, where the beds were forever full. In 1887 the committee acquired a large house in Springfield Place with room for twice the number of cots; it was very soon full so the search was on to procure even more spacious accommodation.

In 1888 a large site at the corner of St Mary's Road and Welbury Drive was acquired and on May 1st 1889, Samuel Cunliffe Lister, aka Lord Masham, laid the foundation stone for a new hospital. At the lunch at the Alexandra Hotel which followed he added that he would give £5,000 towards the required sum of £12,000.

There were 25 cots in each of the two wards arranged in a circle around the room. The only qualification for admission was sickness and poverty. The charity's stated objectives were the medical and surgical treatment of the children of the poor.

A newspaper report in 1897 said that since the start in Hanover Square up to 3,000 children had been treated as in-patients, and between 8,000 and 9,000 outpatients.

The Infirmary grew out of the Bradford Public Dispensary which was founded in 1825; a new dispensary building opened at Darley Street in 1827; in 1833 it became known as Bradford Infirmary; in 1843 the new Bradford Infirmary officially opened for outpatients at Westgate with twelve beds. In 1848 surgeon Edward Casson was the first to operate on a patient in Bradford using a new wonder drug – chloroform which had been demonstrated the previous year. One early disaster it had to deal with was the December 1882 Newlands Mill chimney disaster when a strong gust of wind caused the Mill in Bowling to collapse, resulting in the loss of 54 lives, mostly children.

In 1892 the first officially-trained nurses were appointed and in 1897 work on a new nurses' home for 55 nurses began in the infirmary's grounds in Ivegate. The hospital became the Bradford Royal Infirmary in 1897 in commemoration of Queen Victoria's Diamond Jubilee. In 1927 construction began on the first block of buildings at Duckworth Lane for the new BRI. The current facility moved from Westgate and opened in 1937 in Duckworth Lane.

In 1950 a school of physiotherapy and a thoracic surgical unit opened at BRI while in the next decade BRI made international headlines following pioneering work in the fight against breast cancer by George Whyte Watson and Professor Robert Turner. Their game-changing research into chemotherapy gives the hospital a worldwide reputation for cancer treatment.

*INTERIOR OF MIDLAND STATION, BRADFORD*

The Leeds and Bradford Railway operated the first rail service into Bradford on 1st July 1846. It came in from the north, up Bradford Dale from Shipley, and terminated at a railway station on Kirkgate, opposite the end of Market Street. There were hourly services to Leeds Wellington Station, and through trains to London Euston via Derby and Rugby.

This first railway station was a fine neoclassical building; by 1853, the Midland Railway had acquired the Leeds and Bradford, and rebuilt the station. In 1890, the railway station was again replaced, this time with a large complex comprising the passenger station, goods station and the Midland Hotel, the interior and exterior are illustrated here. In the 60s the station was being called Market Street Station. In 1906, Forster Square was built to the south-east of the railway station, but the name Forster Square Station was not adopted until 1924.

With Boothroyd's Temperance Hotel on the right and St Peter's House and Bradford Cathedral in the centre. Forster Square was laid out in the late-19th century at the bottom of Kirkgate, and named after the 19th-century politician William Edward Forster. Until 1958, it was a spacious city square, triangular in shape, with public gardens and a statue of Forster dominating the centre. Bradford Cathedral (Cathedral Church of St Peter) is built on a site used for Christian worship since the 8th century, when missionaries based in Dewsbury evangelised the area. Until 1919, it was the parish church of St Peter.

William Edward Forster, PC, FRS (1818 – 1886) was an industrialist, philanthropist and Liberal Party statesman. As MP for Bradford and Chief Secretary for Ireland in 1881, he introduced a Coercion Bill in the House of Commons, to deal with the growth of the Land League. Among its provisions was one enabling the Irish government to arrest without trial persons "reasonably suspected" of crime and conspiracy. He was nicknamed "Buckshot" by the Nationalist press, on the supposition that he had ordered its use by the police when firing on a crowd.

Forster caricatured as an ape in *Vanity Fair* 27th February 1869. By Carlo Pellegrini (1839–1889). The caption to the picture read "*If he is not an advanced liberal, it is for want of advancing himself.*"

This fire in the 50s destroyed a warehouse at the junction of Canal Road and Bolton Road. The office block to the rear was mainly occupied by Grattan Warehouses, the famous Bradford mail order catalogue company.

Forster Square changed dramatically in the mid-1960s when the Brutalist blocks of Central House and Forster House photographed here were built. They were part of the redevelopment of central Bradford envisaged by Stanley Wardle's 1953 plan published in the *Development Plan of the County Borough of Bradford*. Only St. Peter's House survived the redevelopment of the square. The blocks were designed by the controversial architect and businessman John Poulson. His corruption trial was a key event in demonstrating the need for the Register of Member's Interests for Parliament. In 2005 the blocks were demolished. It was envisaged that a new shopping centre would be built in the square soon after, but the plan stalled because the project didn't attract enough key tenants. So the site lay empty becoming Bradford's infamous 'Hole in the Ground' until protests encouraged the council to do something. They established a park in April 2010 with seating and a performance area, creating a public space in the square for the first time in decades. For a few brief years, until January 2014, Forster Square was open. In November the following year the Broadway Shopping Centre began trading.

The 3.5 mile long Bradford Canal was built in 1774 to connect the centre of Bradford with the Leeds-Liverpool Canal. Here is the junction of the two at Dockfield, Shipley. Robinson's the boat builders occupied the white-washed building.

The Bradford Canal ran from the Leeds and Liverpool Canal at Shipley along the track of Canal Road into the centre of Bradford. The canal closed in 1866, when it was declared to be a public health hazard. It reopened in 1870 with an improved water supply, only to close for the second time in 1922. On its course it dropped by 86 feet through ten locks.

An Act of Parliament of April 1771 appointed 28 proprietors who were permitted to raise £6,000 in capital by issuing shares, with a further £3,000 if needed, to be used to construct a canal from Shipley to a place in Bradford called Hoppy Bridge Wharf, which is now under Forster Square. They could also build reservoirs, and take water from various brooks. In the early days the principal cargo was stone as a number of kilns were built beside the canal by the Bradford Lime Kiln Company and limestone was brought from Skipton.

Around 1790 the newly-established Bowling Iron Works built a wagon-way from its works in Bowling to a staithes at Golden Lyon Yard about 200 yards south of the canal basin enabling iron products and coal to be exported from the town by the canal via the wagon-way. The carriage of wool from Australia was an important source of revenue from the 1820s, and from 1828, packet boats carried passengers to Selby and Leeds.

The painting is *Old Canal Basin* by A Geller, now in Bradford Art Gallery.

The construction of slum housing and the absence of any sanitation or sewerage systems soon produced a fetid, polluted waterway, described locally as the '*seething cauldron of all impurity, the Bradford Canal*'. The canal finally closed for good in 1922 under an Act of Abandonment.

Town Hall Square, Bradford

Bradford City Hall is built in the Venetian style, 19th-century and stands in Centenary Square, famous for its landmark bell-clock tower, modelled on the campanile on the Palazzo Vecchio – Florence's city hall. It houses 13 bells, installed in 1872, which weigh over 13 tons and first rang at the opening in 1873. All the original bells are still in use but the carillon mechanism has been updated several times

Before the city hall was built the town hall was the Fire Station House in Swain Street between 1847 and 1872. In 1869, a new triangular site was purchased, and a competition held for a design to rival the town halls of Leeds and Halifax. It was first extended in 1909 with another council chamber, more committee rooms and a banqueting hall. It was extended again in 1914 with a new entrance and staircase in baroque marble and listed grade I on 14th June 1963.

The 35 statues of past monarchs stand sentinel in chronological order on the façade, with Queen Victoria and Elizabeth I on either side of the main entrance. All are carved from Cliffe Wood stone, from the local quarry on Bolton Road. On the side facing Centenary Square, the line of monarchs includes Oliver Cromwell who, of course, was never a monarch. Irish workers declined to take part in fitting the statue of Cromwell. William and Mary were joint monarchs from 1689 to 1694 but Mary seemingly did not warrant a statue.

The Kirkgate looking towards Sunbridge Road. Kirkgate Market is on the right. Beyond it with B and B displayed vertically on the building is Brooke Bond's Yorkshire Tea Warehouse. On the left A. Walker's Grand Mantle Warehouse sold mantles, capes, cloaks, coats, jackets and waterproofs.

Tyrell Street from the junction with Sunbridge Road. The Grand Clothing hall stands at the corner of Ivegate.

Another Italianate building at the key junction of Kirkgate, Westgate and Ivegate. The ground floor tenants were jewellers Manoah Rhodes; the windows on each floor are of different designs.

The Mechanics' Institute Library (below) is a splendid four storey classical building which stood between Tyrrel, Bridge and Market Streets. The ground floor housed shops while the Institute, opposite the City Hall, was on the upper floors. It was founded in 1832 and included Thackeray and Ruskin amongst its guests. Opened in 1871; demolished 1971. For over 70 years the Institute played a leading role in adult education in Bradford, providing books, classes and later, a series of popular public lectures.

The first institute was founded by radicals in 1825 but soon folded due to the unpopularity of their views amongst the middle classes. A group of non-conformists and businessmen successfully revived the Institute in the 1830s led by 26 year old Baptist Joseph Farrar, along with Titus Salt and others. it opened its first premises in March, 1832 in Piccadilly and by 1839 moved to larger premises in Wells Street.

The Institute responded to the city's status as an international centre of the worsted cloth industry and the resulting huge demand in Bradford for education in technical and commercial subjects, chemistry (for the dyeing industry), building construction and industrial art and design. Modern languages teaching was also key : it was said that on the Bradford Wool Exchange it was possible to hear every European language on any morning of the week.

The Education Act 1902 empowered local authorities to co-ordinate the work of all the educational bodies in its area. Thus William Forster, Bradford MP and founder member of the Mechanics' Institute, laid the foundations for its demise as a provider of education. In 1904 it was agreed that all classes at the Institute should be transferred to the control of the council through the recently-established Bradford Technical College.

The aim of mechanics' institutes was to provide a technical education for the working man and for professionals: to 'address societal needs by incorporating fundamental scientific thinking and research into engineering solutions'. They transformed science and technology education for the man in the street. The world's first opened in Edinburgh in 1821 as the School of Arts of Edinburgh, later to become Heriot-Watt University; this was followed in 1823 by the Institute in Glasgow which was founded on the site of the institution set up in 1800 by George Birkbeck and the Andersonian University offering free lectures on arts, science and technical subjects; it moved to London in 1804, became The London Mechanics' Institute from 1823 and, later, Birkbeck College. Liverpool opened in July 1823 and Manchester (later to become UMIST) in 1824. By 1850, there were over 700 institutes in the UK and abroad, many of which developed into libraries, colleges and universities.

Mechanics' institutes were a product of the Industrial Revolution during which, as 'a consequence of the introduction of machinery a class of workmen emerged to build, maintain and repair the machines on which the blessing of progress depended, at a time when population shifts and the dissolving influences of industrialization in the new urban areas, where these were concentrated, destroyed the inadequate old apprentice system and threw into relief the connection between material advancement and the necessity of education to take part in its advantages'.

Mechanics' institutes provided free lending libraries and also offered lectures, laboratories, and occasionally, as with Glasgow, a museum.

Bradford Mechanics' Institute was founded in 1832. The city acquired a School of Design in 1848, a School of Building in 1867, and a Weaving School (Bradford Technical School) in 1878. The first building for the new Bradford Technical School was opened in 1882. The Technical College has its origins in this Mechanics' Institute, founded in 1832, formed in response to the need in the city for workers with skills relevant to the workplace. In 1882, the institute became the Bradford Technical School. In 1957, the Bradford Institute of Technology, was formed as a College of Advanced Technology to take on the running of higher education courses.

Cartwright Hall in Lister Park; Bradford's art gallery, built on the former site of Manningham Hall. The gallery opened in 1904 initially with a display of artworks loaned from other galleries and private collections until it was able to purchase a permanent collection of Victorian and Edwardian works using money raised by the 1904 Bradford Exhibition. Since the mid-1980s the Bradford museum group has had a policy to collect works that chime with the cultural background of many of the post-war migrants to the Bradford area. Acquisitions include contemporary South Asian Art – Islamic calligraphy, phulkari style illustrated textiles and items of contemporary Sikh art.

Edmund Cartwright FSA (1743 – 1823) invented the power loom, thereby changing the industrial landscape in the UK completely. In 1784, Cartwright had visited Richard Arkwright's cotton-spinning mills at Cromford in Derbyshire and was compelled by what he had seen to construct a similar machine for weaving. His idea was scorned by many. Cartwright also patented a wool combing machine in 1789 and a cordelier (machine for making rope) in 1792. He also designed interlocking bricks, incombustible floorboards and a steam engine that used alcohol instead of water.

This truly beautiful mosque is in Horton Park Avenue and is one of about 100 in the Bradford area catering for an estimated 130,000 Muslims in Bradford, nearly one quarter of the population (24.7%) of 534,300. In 1983 a four- storey old textile mill was acquired and modernised into this mosque and community centre. It was funded by voluntary contributions, interest-free loans and donations from the local community and membership. It is used regularly by some 3,000 people monthly, participating in various activities and events.

Wool may be long gone from this magnificent building but it has in part been replaced by a bookshop run by Waterstones. The Wool Exchange Building is a grade I listed building built as a wool-trading centre between 1864 and 1867; the grandeur of its Gothic Revival architecture symbolises the wealth and importance that wool brought to Bradford.

Verbal contract only was permitted on the floor of the Exchange, each party keeping a separate note of the price, quantity and delivery date. Members only (holding tickets authorised by the Committee, usually sponsored by an employing firm) were allowed on the trading floor, but there was a walkway around the floor where freelance salesmen and independent traders were allowed to wait in an attempt to catch a member's eye and close a deal "*off floor*". With "*Off floor*" you took your chance on the wool delivered being up to sample; all "*on floor*" deals involved the wool being delivered via the conditioning house on Canal Road where the wool was checked for quality (staple length) and dry weight, since adding water was a popular swindle. To be a member – to "*have a ticket*" – was a social distinction in the old wool-trading world in Bradford.

Spinks' restaurant in a semi-basement below was just as important socially. Almost as much trading and networking went on in these two rooms as on the floor upstairs. The restaurant was open to the public, not just to members, and a hub for Bradford business life in general.

*[17th September 2013, Author Casliber.*
*This file is licensed under the Creative Commons Attribution-Share Alike 3.0 Unported license.]*

Lister's Mill, or Manningham Mills, was the largest silk factory in the world. Samuel Cunliffe Lister built it in 1873 in the Italianate style to replace the original Manningham Mills after it was burnt to the ground in 1871. In its heyday 11,000 men, women and children were working at Lister's – all busy making top end textiles such as velvet and silk. In 1911 the firm supplied 1,000 yards of velvet for George V's Coronation and in 1976 new velvet curtains for President Ford at the White House.

Lister's played a role in the formation of the Independent Labour Party with the 1890–91 strike at the mill. When US import tariffs began to impact on the bottom line Lister's simply and capriciously used the expedient of posting a notice in the mill announcing the intention to cut the wages of 1,100 workers by 25% in the run up to Christmas, and threatening to lock out those who refused. The Victorian equivalent of human resources by e- mail. The shambolic but determined workforce was furious and at its height the strike saw 5,000 workers downing tools from December to April with riots in the streets midst futile attempts to negotiate a settlement.

Silk spinning in the mill, 1984.   *Photo by Ian Beesley*

The earliest records show that Bradford Grammar School was already flourishing in the mid-sixteenth century. In 1662 the school was re-established by Royal Charter as the Free Grammar School of Charles II at Bradford. In 1949 the school moved from the city centre to its present site at Frizinghall.

# Bradford celebrates

The people of Bradford responded to the Coronation of Edward VII with a huge bonfire in Allerton. One solitary policeman (*below*) has been detailed to provide security and maintain law and order.

On May 4th 1904 the Prince of Wales, the future George V, came to Bradford to unveil the statue of his late grandmother, Queen Victoria; this is how the city reacted: they packed Victoria Square. The statue is twelve foot high and weighs three tons in bronze depicting the queen as she looked at her Golden Jubilee in 1887. Victoria signed off Bradford as a city in 1897 and signed the Charter of Incorporation uniting the townships of Bradford, Manningham, Bowling and Horton.

When Samuel Lister saw the state that Manningham Hall, his boyhood home, had fallen into after its purchase from him by Bradford Corporation he was appalled. So, he bought the shabby hall back and had Cartwright Hall built as a permanent memorial to Edmund Cartwright and as an impressive art gallery.

At the turn of the century something was needed to boost Bradford's ailing reputation as a prominent place for trade and industry, 'to show that Bradford's textile goods were still among the best in the world and at the same time to remind visitors that the city had other strings to its bow'. This was the plan:

twenty-three acres, about two-thirds of the area of the park, was to be enclosed by an unclimbable fence, ten feet high. An Industrial Hall, three hundred feet long and about a hundred and eighty feet wide, made of corrugated iron and wood, with six transepts was to be built. The textile industry was to occupy the main hall, with demonstrations of every process of manufacture up to the finished garment. It was arranged that the centrepiece of this section should be a Dress Show put on by ten leading firms, all household names, such as Drummond's, John Foster's, A & S Henry's, and, of course, Titus Salt's. The Bradford Dyers' Association were also to have a stand.

- *http://www.bradfordhistorical.org.uk/cartwright.html*

Other industries were represented in the wings: mining, locomotives, engineering, machinery, sanitation, recreation and science; there was also a special section devoted to women's work : art and craft, domestic exhibits and education. A kitchen was the place for cookery demonstrations. All in all there were 145 separate displays with famous names such as Fattorini & Sons, Chivers, Brown and Polson, Jones's Sewing Machines, Cumberland Pencils, Cadbury's, and Pilkington's represented. The lake hosted a mock battle in which boats representing the Russian and Japanese fleets clashed, reference to the actual war taking place between the Russian Empire and the Empire of Japan – the Russo-Japanese War of 1904 and 1905 over rival imperial claims on Manchuria and Korea.

The Exhibition was opened on May 4th 1904 by the Prince and Princess of Wales (the future King George V and Queen Mary). At the opening this cabinet, with each drawer containing three samples of finest fabric from a different Bradford manufaturer, was presented to the Princess of Wales. The exhibition went on all summer and into the autumn, closing on 29th October. Some details: 21,640 season tickets were sold at 10/6d each (half-price after August); a 'package deal' of entrance tickets with railway excursion fares sold over 17,000. On 20th July the millionth visitor, a farmer from the Dales, was presented with a medallion, and the two-millionth visitor, Thomas Lee of Otley Road, was awarded a gold watch and chain. The total attendance was 2,417,928 with a record attendance of 64,847 on the final day. Total receipts from ticket sales were £41,828 and with money raised from sale of some of the buildings the final profit was £14,965. Half went to the Libraries, Museums and Art Galleries Fund, chiefly towards the cost of buying a permanent art collection.

The most popular attraction was the Bradford Industrial Exhibition Hall quickly followed by the Water Chute from Canada which stood on the edge of the lake with twenty small shops representing Old Bradford under its structure. Then there was the Palace of Illusions:

> "a many-sided chamber with mirrored walls and Gothic arches stretching on either hand, apparently for miles. The lights would dim, and then suddenly there would be simultaneous illumination of brilliant electric lights on each pillar, which would give the illusion of thousands of lights. Then would follow a mystifying dance by a beautiful lady artiste, which, reflected in hundreds of mirrors, would give the impression of a large ballet".

There was also a Crystal Maze caused by distorting mirrors, a Gravity Railway and The Gigantic Glittering Thimble, 9 feet 6 inches high, 'the world's largest'. There were swimming carnivals, Swedish drill displays and target practice on a rifle range. A dog show brought in nearly 1,000 entries.

The lake was spanned by the Japanese inspired Fairy Bridge crossed by way of one of the islands over its north end. The end of the Canadian water chute can just be seen under the bridge's span on the left. The oriental theme was continued elsewhere...

Approaching the Concert Hall was a perfect avenue of lanterns: it was almost like a Japanese Feast of Lanterns … No fewer than 5,000 fairy lamps and 5,000 Chinese lanterns are employed.

Musical entertainment was central to the event with performances by The Blue Hungarian Band, a Ladies' Orchestra, the Eastbrook Choir, the Bradford Festival and Old Choral Societies, and the Crosland Moor Handbell Ringers. There were choirs from Bradford schools, some with up to 400 singers, conjuring and 'animated pictures'; the bands of the Coldstream Guards, the Scots Guards and the Life Guards. And, top of the bill: the Black Dyke Mills Band.

An innovative display was a Model Hospital where nursing skills were demonstrated; and a nursery, where visitors could leave their young children. A Baby Incubator was of particular fascination, used to demonstrate how the lives of premature babies could be saved in those days of high infant mortality.

The Somali village stole the show, although it only got booked when the Ashanti village cancelled at short notice. The 100 or so Somalis, with their chief, included, according to the *Yorkshire Daily Observer*, 'remarkably beautiful girls'. They all arrived before the Exhibition got under way, built their own huts and lived in them giving daily demonstrations of dancing, spear throwing and shooting arrows. According to the official report, 'they maintained their attractive character throughout, and under the trying conditions of the Yorkshire climate behaved in a most creditable manner'. Apparently they spent much of their time huddled round oil stoves. One of their huts was destroyed by fire, and one of the women died and was buried in Scholemoor Cemetery.

On 13th September a daughter was born to the head of the Somalis, the Sultan Ali and his wife, Fatima. The baby was aptly given the name of Hadija Yorkshire and in honour of the occasion a salute of 17 guns was fired from Port Arthur by Lieutenant Lot Morgan.

[The performers] faced the disadvantages of drenching rain and slippery turf with commendable pluck.

That's how the *Yorkshire Evening Post* on July 14th 1931 described the opening of the Bradford Historical Pageant the day before. Nevertheless, the show went on and provided some much needed colour and gaiety in the teeth of the most devastating depression of the 20th century when, in Bradford, an industrial city heavily dependent on exports, tens of thousands of workers were unemployed and wages were being slashed for those lucky enough to have jobs. Between 1928 and 1932, nearly 400 textile firms in the city went bankrupt.

Parts of the above are based on *Cartwright Memorial Hall and the Great Bradford Exhibition of 1904* by Anne Bishop. (First published in 1989 in volume 4, pp. 26-38, of the third series of *The Bradford Antiquary*, the journal of the Bradford Historical and Antiquarian Society.)

That the pageant was to serve as a commercial advertisement for the city was reflected in the drama itself. In the Prologue, a shepherdess standing in the middle of a flock of sheep, sets up the entire narrative inside a textile metaphor:

> As my cloth is woven from the wool I know so well, so today, in this great city of industry, my aim is to weave for you a story that shall be like a beautiful fabric […] a tapestry of many colours and many figures that will please the eye and linger in your memory.

The first episode begins with the arrival of the Romans.

The text moves through the production of woollen textiles, from the flock of sheep in the prologue, to a sheep-shearing spectacle and song set at Kirkstall Abbey in the Norman episode, to a "spinning chorus" … at the start of the fourth episode (right) … at the end of episode three the audience hears resounding cries of "Who'll buy?" in a depiction of the establishment of Bradford's wool market — but it marks the start of the story of the city's textile industry and its commercial success. The rest of the pageant is full of what we might now call "product placements" by the wool industry, from a scene showing men stuffing the Lord Chancellor's "woolsack" with Bradford wool to girls enthusing over silk ribbon, a famous Bradford product, in the final episode.

The Bolling Hall ghost in Episode V recreated the episode during the English Civil War when the spectre saved the townsfolk from a massacre. It appeared in the bedroom of the Royalist Earl of Newcastle wringing it's hands and saying *'Pity poor Bradford'*. The Earl was so unnerved by the apparition that after defeating the town's defenders he spared the populace, instead of punishing the Parliamentary town as he originally intended.

The pageant was seen as an attempt to revive the commercial fortunes of the city; the opening speech, delivered by Prince George (later the Duke of Kent), was unequivocal, saying the pageant would *"increase the prosperity of the city and help to promote the revival of its trade,"*. The theme runs through other speeches. The original idea for the pageant had been to provide a cultural complement to an industrial fair, the Imperial Wool Industries Fair, held the same month at Bradford's Olympia Hall.

Making the props for the pageant in local schools, the students below are manoeuvring the Saxon cross for Episode II. Bradford was one of the first major pageants to make extensive use of electricity. Telephone lines were set up to convey announcements more expediently to the large number of participants, and microphones

were used to make the outdoor drama easier to hear. A microphone was also installed for the first time in Bradford Cathedral to broadcast the Archbishop of York's pageant sermon.

Throughout the drama, thousands of performers dressed in garments made with local textiles served as a living advertisement for Bradford's industry and, according to the *Yorkshire Observer*'s souvenir programme, the production of this spectacle was a quasi-industrial process, involving the transformation of more than 25,000 yards of "multi-coloured materials into the gayest and biggest variety of costumes Bradford has ever seen.

All pageant images and elements of the text courtesy of The Redress of the Past and Dr Paul Readman, King's College London.

*http://www.historicalpageants.ac.uk/featured-pageants/bradford-pageant-1931/*

# Bad Bradford Days

In Bradford the worst night of the Second World War was 31st August 1940, when 120 high explosive bombs fell on the city. The raid began at 11.13pm and ended at 2.40am. Lingard's department store in Westgate was a casualty as was the British Shoe Co. next door and the Kirkgate Chapel round the corner; 10,000 windows in the city were smashed. Although 100 people were injured there was only one fatality, a woman. There were, however, some close shaves: fortunately the auditorium in the Odeon cinema had just cleared when a bomb came through the roof and landed in the stalls. Another bomb in Tyrrel Street just missed people waiting for a tram.

The *Telegraph & Argus* reported on four raids altogether between August 22nd 1940 and March 14th 1941. The first saw three bombs fall on Heaton Woods; the second was four bombs which caused minimal damage and six injuries; the third was the August 1940 raid. The *Telegraph & Argus* reported that the city endured an even heavier bombardment on 14th March 1941 when 595 bombs rained down – again casualties and damage were slight. It seems that there are no other records to substantiate this event.

Many Bradford children were evacuated to Nelson in Lancashire or to other West Riding towns like Mirfield and Harrogate. For the Jewish children arriving at a Manningham hostel in 1939, it was the other way round: Bradford was a place of refuge.

Lives were also lost when planes crashed into houses. Three died and five were seriously injured when a German bomber hit a row of four cottages in Idle. The crew were taken prisoners of war.

Looms were working at full capacity making cloth for uniforms or other war purposes – Lister's mill in Manningham made material for parachutes. Jowett's, the car makers, expanded its workforce four-fold, many of the new staff being women.

In Rawson Place Market, John Street, 32 stalls and seven street-facing shops were wrecked.

Nothing like a good crash to draw a crowd of gawpers... A crashed Ford Model T (also known as the Tin Lizzie, T-Model Ford, Model T, T, Leaping Lena, or Flivver) in Bradford in 1929. Car wheels were initially wooden artillery wheels, with steel welded-spoke wheels only available in 1926 and 1927. Flat tyres were always a problem and a hazard due to the plethora of horseshoe nails on the roads and the high pressure required for the tyres. In the twelve years between the end of the First World War and 1930 the number of cars on Britain's roads increased from 200,000 to one million; between the two world wars a staggering 120,000 people were killed in road accidents.

An increasingly familiar sight – these were the floods which struck Bradford city centre in 1968. The weather station in Lister Park measured 0.88 inches (22 mm) of rain fell in 30 minutes. Bradford Beck overflowed into the torrential streets.

A tram accident in Bradford in July 1907. Bradford City Tramways tram No. 210 derailed in Church Bank due to a fractured axle. Two people were killed and sixteen were injured. This followed another accident which occurred at Four Lane Ends, Allerton on the Bradford Tramways & Omnibus Co's system on December 4th 1889. The *Yorkshire Post* reported the death of one person and injury, four seriously, to several others. The car had become detached from the engine when operating from Bradford to Allerton, and ran back down an incline until, on reaching a curve, it parted company with the rails and fell on its side. Of the nine in the car, several escaped unhurt or with very slight injuries.

In 1917 Bernard Stuttard, a wool warehouseman at John Cure & Co Ltd, died from anthrax poisoning. What became known as the 'Bradford Disease' was not an uncommon occupational disease in the area with its heavy reliance on the wool and fleece industry.

Bradford, but sadly not Mr Stuttard, was lucky to have a Dr Friederich Wilhem Eurich (1869-1945), born in Chemnitz, a major textile centre in Saxony, working at the Bradford Royal Infirmary from 1896 where he held a Saturday morning surgery, free of charge, later moving on to the Pathological and Bacteriological Laboratory in the Technical College as bacteriologist. Eurich had come to Bradford when his father moved to the branch of a German yarn firm in Little Germany.

Late in 1905 the Bradford Anthrax Investigation Board relocated the laboratory to Morley Street with Eurich as bacteriologist with no regard for his own health and at great risk while investigating the disease. The Board instituted other medical measures against anthrax and, in 1918, built a Wool Disinfecting Station in Liverpool, the port where all dangerous wools and skins had to come through.

His focus was on the elimination of the deadly anthrax (wool sorters' disease) caused by a spore-forming bacterium, Bacillus anthracis which can infect humans by contact with blood from an infected animal. His pioneering work led to a cure for the disease which saved thousands of lives.

The Bradford Sweets Poisoning of 1858 was the accidental arsenic poisoning of more than 200 people. Twenty people died and over 200 became seriously ill when sweets inadvertently made with arsenic were sold from a market stall in Bradford. For centuries before, sugar was extremely expensive and was called "white gold". The government recognised the opportunities here and taxed it severely: in 1815 the tax raised from sugar in Britain was £3,000,000. To defray the costs of raw materials, sweet and chocolate manufacturers resorted to adulteration and their products were often mixed with cheaper, substances or 'daft'. 'Daft' was a concoction of harmless substances such as powdered limestone and plaster of Paris.

William Hardaker, known locally as "Humbug Billy", routinely sold his sweets from a stall in the Green Market in Bradford; his supplier, Joseph Neal, the manufacturer of the sweets – including peppermint humbugs – used 'daft' in his sweet production, 'daft' that was supplied by a druggist in Shipley. Tragically, twelve pounds of arsenic trioxide were sold instead of the harmless 'daft'. Both 'daft' and arsenic trioxide are white powders and look alike; the arsenic trioxide was not properly labelled and negligently stored next to the 'daft'.

The mistake went undiscovered during the manufacture of the sweets: Appleton combined forty pounds of sugar, twelve pounds of arsenic trioxide, four pounds of gum, and peppermint oil, to make forty pounds of peppermint humbugs. The sweets contained enough arsenic to kill two people per humbug.

THE GREAT LOZENGE-MAKER.
A Hint to Paterfamilias.

As usual, Hardaker sold the poisoned sweets from his stall. Of those who bought and ate the sweets, around twenty people died, with a further 200 or so becoming severely ill with arsenic poisoning within a day or so. All involved in the production and sale were charged with manslaughter, but none were convicted. How? Because there was no law in place that made food adulteration illegal.

Good did, however, come from this tragedy: there was new legislation to protect the public in the form of the 1860 Adulteration of Food and Drink Bill which changed the way in which ingredients could be used, mixed and combined. The UK Pharmacy Act of 1868 introduced more stringent regulations regarding the handling and selling of named poisons and medicines by pharmacists. The abolition of the sugar tax in 1874 meant sugar became affordable to all, thus making 'daft' redundant.

The 'Great Lozenge Maker' cartoon by John Leach (1817-1864) was published in *Punch* on November 22nd 1858. 'A Hint to Paterfamilias' – is a warning to parents about the potential dangers of treating their children to sweets. Reinforcing this message comes with the box titled 'BON-BONS FOR JUVENILE PARTIES' on the top-shelf. Before the Bradford case, the Select Committee on the Adulteration of Food, Drink and Drugs, formed by Parliament in the summer of 1855, revealed that sweets were made brightly coloured by using toxic minerals. A vivid green, for instance, was achieved by using copper acetoarsenite, an arsenic compound.

The Low Moor Ironworks in the early 1900s. The carts in the centre ground were pulled by horses. Note how close the houses are to the plant. Things started to change dramatically in Bradford around 1788; before then, Low Moor, three miles south of Bradford, was nothing more than a hamlet supporting a handful of cottages in which handloom weavers toiled away, selling their produce in Halifax Piece Hall and similar places. That was before Low Moor Ironworks and its wrought iron foundries were established and expanded rapidly to become a global name in the production and export of wrought iron and its products from 1801 until 1957. Low Moor was one of five principal steel works in Bradford, the others being Emmetts (1782), Bowling (1788), Shelf (1792) and Bierley (1811).

Low Moor Explosion. August 21st 1916

21st August 1916 was the day of one of the UK's worst industrial disasters, at Low Moor Munitions Company, ('Factory No 182, Yorkshire') – the Low Moor Chemical Company before the war, at the bottom of New Works Road. Here, large amounts of picric acid, a constituent used in the making of high explosives, was being manufactured. Also known as lyddite – after Lydd, in Kent, where the initial acceptance trials were made, the acid also comes in yellow dye form and is used in the manufacture of carpets.

On that fateful day, the factory housed 30,000lb of picric acid which was awaiting tests and then shipment. More was still being processed and in transit from the drying sheds to the lower magazine. At 2.30pm a worker was moving picric acid across the yard when he heard a hissing sound; there was no fire alarm, the water sprinklers were on but no one could remember if any water was ever sprinkled. What everyone did know was that a huge explosion was imminent.

Ten minutes later that explosion came, sending up a fireball. It was heard as far away as York some forty miles distant; debris rained down all around and the smell of bad eggs filled the air. Despite the valiant efforts of the works fire brigade to bring the resulting inferno under control, the fire continued unrestrained. When the first of the Bradford firemen arrived from Odsal station, a huge explosion blew them completely off the engine and, in the words of Chief Officer Scott: *"within half an hour of turning out to the fire, all eighteen men were in the infirmary or killed."* The Odsal engine was crushed under a wall killing two firemen.

Further explosions, large and minor, kept coming, scattering blazing debris all over the place and soon the whole works were destroyed. At nearby North Bierley Works in Cleckheaton Road, a large gasometer containing 270,000 cubic feet (7,600 m$^3$) of gas was ruptured by cascading debris. The escaping gas soon ignited, the exploding heat was felt almost a mile away and the noise rendered one seven year old boy deaf. War time censorship ensured that no mention of the disaster was reported by the press.

In the railway sidings almost thirty carriages and wagons were destroyed and 100 others seriously damaged. The shattered remains of the signal box are pictured above. The casualties were rushed to hospital in handcarts. The explosions continued for two days: it was three days before the fire was extinguished completely. People had to stay with friends, family, some slept in woods, or sheltered in schools. Three schools were forced to close. Houses and shops within a two mile radius had their windows smashed and roofs damaged, ceilings caved in and doors destroyed. Some properties were totally demolished by the explosion and twenty-nine houses in First Street were built in 1919 as replacements. Terrified dogs fled the scene, some later found as far away as Wakefield, Huddersfield and Halifax. Thirty-four people were killed and sixty injured in the works. Outside the works, many more were injured by flying shards of glass and debris.

Until 1935 smallpox was endemic in the UK: for example, 1902 saw 2,600 deaths; its scarcity after it was largely eradicated unfortunately led to slow diagnosis and sometimes misdiagnosis. In January 1962 this led to an outbreak in Bradford. The picture shows orderly queues outside St George's Hall waiting for vaccination. The following is taken from the *Hansard* report, HC Deb 15th February 1962 vol 653 cc1655-66:

**Mr. Arthur Tiley (Bradford, West):** Bradford has a population of 300,000. The disease began when a Pakistani child died on 30th December. Unfortunately the death was returned as malaria. This is why the position was grave, because for many days smallpox was in our midst but not detected… I am instructed by our Medical Officer of Health to say that the Pakistanis co-operated in every way possible in the work he did in seeking out contacts and isolating them. There were fourteen definite cases in Bradford. There were six deaths. There was one death in addition to the six which was partly due to smallpox. Therefore, we were dealing with a very virulent type of germ. The death rate amongst those affected was very high.

Inside five days the authorities in my city vaccinated between 250,000 and 275,000 people. In addition, in the 24 hours following the first indication of the disease they sought out 900 direct contacts. That was the great danger. Normally, the contacts are few, but here hospitals, a slaughterhouse and visitors to hospitals were involved. In all, for about three weeks 900 people were visited daily and subject to medical check and watched for any sign of the disease.

The 2020 Coronavirus taught us all quite a lot about disease prevention, contagion control, self-isolation and social distancing. But, for those who care to look back, so did the flu epidemic which scourged the UK in the winter of 1932-1933. The article shows how Bradford City players distanced themselves and continued to exercise by walking the North Cliffs at Blackpool, imbibing the unpolluted air, and how the Bradford Park Avenue team mass gargled as a precaution against the disease. Lister's Mill was sprayed with disinfectant and workers were offered a gargle.

# Bradford's People

The portrait of Frederick Delius which hangs in Bolling Hall; and the sculpture erected in honour of Delius in Exchange Square.

Frederick Theodore Albert Delius (29th January 1862 – 10th June 1934 – originally Friederich, commonly known as Frederick, Fred to close friends and Fritz to his family – was born in Claremont, Bradford, to a German wool merchant and his wife. Delius never really liked Bradford, nor did he much like English music, retorting once that he'd never actually heard any. Delius attended Bradford Grammar School; his parents had hopes for him in the wool trade but their son was having none of it – he wanted to be a musician. He was sent to Florida in 1884 to manage an orange plantation but soon tired of oranges and in 1886 returned to Europe.

Delius soon made it to Leipzig, birthplace of Wagner and a centre of German culture and music. He later settled in Paris where he contracted syphilis which, from 1918, left him blind and paralyzed. He had moved to Grez-sur-Loing some 70 km south of Paris near Fontainebleau, a place notable for the artists and musicians who congregated there. Delius, however, apart from being paralyzed and blind had the added problem that he was tone death. The composer Eric Fenby, himself from Scarborough, offered his services as an amanuensis and between the two of them, despite the difficulties, worked out a way of delivering much of Delius's music to the world. Fenby was artistic director for the 1962 Bradford Delius Festival.

Delius died in 1934 – the same year as Holst and Elgar; a wreath made from heather from Baildon Moor – a favourite haunt of Delius's – was sent to the funeral from the Lord Mayor and citizens of Bradford.

The sculpture, *A Quatrefoil for Delius*, by Amber Hiscott, was unveiled in Delius's honour, in Exchange Square, Bradford, on 23 November 1993. A quatrefoil is defined as an ornamental design of four lobes or leaves as used in architectural tracery, resembling a flower or clover leaf.

*Images courtesy and © Bradford Telegraph & Argus*

Isabella Ormston Ford (1855–1924), social reformer, suffragist, socialist propagandist and writer, was not born in Bradford, but born in leafy St John's Hill, Clarendon Road, Headingley, Leeds, the youngest of eight children of Quakers Robert Lawson Ford and Hannah (née Pease). Nevertheless, Isabella did significant work in Bradford working for women's and workers' rights amongst the mill girls.

Ever at the cutting edge, Isabella Ford worked tirelessly amongst tailoresses who were campaigning for improved working conditions. In 1889 she established the Leeds Tailoresses' Union and the following year she was elected president. In 1890 she marched with workers from Manningham Mills as part of the 19 week Manningham Mills strike of Bradford textile workers. A month after the dispute ended, Bradford Labour Union was formed, and the Independent Labour Party was set up in Bradford in 1893. During the 1890s Isabella was active in propaganda work for the ILP all over the West Riding of Yorkshire,
speaking *"often at street corners, in dingy club rooms, in hot, crowded school rooms"*. (*Bradford Pioneer*, July 1924). Ford's name and image, and those of 58 other women's suffrage supporters, are etched on the plinth of the statue of Millicent Fawcett in Parliament Square, London unveiled in 2018.

'The Morning Wash' – Bradford's Back to the Land Pioneers during the First World War. The various Back-To-The-Land movements encouraged people to take up smallholding and to grow food from the land on a small-scale basis, either for themselves or for third parties.

The Bradford Pals were three First World War Pals battalions of Kitchener's Army raised in the city. The battalions were officially designated the 16th (1st Bradford), 18th (2nd Bradford), and 20th (Reserve) Battalions, and The Prince of Wales's Own (West Yorkshire Regiment).

On the fateful morning of 1st July 1916, the 16th and 18th Battalions climbed out of their trenches to advance across no man's land. It was the first hour of the first day of the Battle of the Somme. Of the estimated 1,394 men from Bradford and District in the two battalions, 1,060 were either killed or injured during the ill-fated attack on the village of Serre-lès-Puisieux.

Other Bradford battalions of the Prince of Wales's Own at the Somme were the 1st/6th Battalion (the former Bradford Rifle Volunteers), part of the Territorial Force, based at Belle Vue Barracks in Manningham, and the 10th Battalion. The 1/6th Battalion first saw action in 1915 at the Battle of Aubers Ridge before moving north to the Yser Canal near Ypres. On the first day of the Somme they too took heavy casualties while trying to support the 36th (Ulster) Division. The 10th Battalion was involved in the attack on Fricourt, where it suffered the highest casualty rate of any battalion on the Somme on 1st July and perhaps the highest battalion casualty list for a single day during the entire war. Nearly 60% of the battalion's casualties were fatal.

The 1/2nd and 2/2nd West Riding Brigades, Royal Field Artillery (TF), had their HQ at Valley Parade in Manningham, with batteries at Bradford, Halifax and Heckmondwike. The 1/2nd Brigade crossed to France with the 1/6th Battalion West Yorks in April 1915. These Territorial Force units were to remain close to each other throughout the war, serving in the 49th (West Riding) Division. They were joined in 1917 by the 2/6th Battalion, West Yorks, and 2/2nd West Riding Brigade, RFA, serving in the 62nd (2nd West Riding) Division.

Pals regiments had proved a tragic and costly disaster: few of the recruits came home again – the economic and social impact alone on their communities after 1918 was incalculable. Well-meaning the idea may have been by the donkeys back in HQ, but the ugly words 'cannon fodder' spring to mind with justification when we contemplate the wholesale slaughter of these particular lions.

The 'Avenge Hartlepool' poster refers to the raid on Hartlepool and West Hartlepool very early in the First World War. When the German Imperial Fleet bombarded the town causing numerous casualties – dead and injures – and mass destruction of the town's housing stock. For full detail see the author's *Old Hartlepool* also published by Stenlake Publishing.

Jonathan Silver was born in Bradford, and was a pupil at Bradford Grammar School. His interest in David Hockney's art grew after they met at Silver's father's burger bar; Hockney agreed to design a cover for the school magazine. Silver then went on to study Art History and Textiles at Leeds University.

Silver would spend his school lunch breaks at the local auction rooms buying and selling furniture. By 1979 he had 13 menswear shops nationwide as well as a clothing factory, Noble Crest, and a shop called Art and Furniture in Manchester.

We have the admirable Jonathan Silver to thank for many things. First he saved Salt Mills in Saltaire from rapid dereliction in 1987 when he bought it for £500,000, thus conserving a magnificent piece of industrial and Yorkshire history; second, he spent thousands more restoring inside and out to make it into one of the country's leading art galleries and art spaces; third, he bought 56 of David Hockney's art works and displayed them in the former spinning room with a grand opening in 1987.

Sadly, Jonathan Silver died in 1987 but Salts Mill continues to thrive today as one of the major arts, cultural and commercial venue in the north of England. The work done by Jonathan Silver in reviving Salts Mill played a large part in

Saltaire village becoming a UNESCO World Heritage Site in December 2001.

*Image courtesy and © Bradford Telegraph & Argus.*

Hockney was born in Bradford to Laura and Kenneth Hockney (a conscientious objector in the Second World War), the fourth of five children. He was educated at Wellington Primary School, Bradford Grammar School, Bradford College of Art and the Royal College of Art in London.

He moved to Los Angeles in 1964, but returned frequently to Yorkshire in the 1990s, usually every three months, to visit his mother who died in 1999. He rarely stayed for more than two weeks until 1997, when his friend Jonathan Silver who was terminally ill encouraged him to capture the local surroundings in his art. He did this at first with paintings based on memory, some from his boyhood. In 1998, he completed the painting of the Yorkshire landmark, Garrowby Hill. Hockney was returning to Yorkshire for longer and longer stays, and by 2003 was painting the countryside *en plein air* in both oils and watercolor. He set up home and a studio in a converted bed and breakfast, in Bridlington. Hockney's largest painting, *Bigger Trees Near Warter or/ou Peinture sur le Motif pour le Nouvel Age Post-Photographique*, which measures 15 feet by 40 feet, was hung in the Royal Academy. This work "is a monumental-scale view of a coppice between Bridlington and York. It was painted on 50 individual canvases, mostly working in situ, over five weeks. He donated it to the Tate.

# Miracle at the mill

**Monday, November 2, 1987**

Salts Mill was closed in February 1986, after 133 years as a textile factory. For months the 17-acre site lay neglected. The state of Sir Titus Salt's pride and joy was reflected in the worsening condition of his surrounding model village.

On June 10, 1987, the mill was purchased for under £500,000 from the Illingworth Morris company by Bradford-born entrepreneur and art lover Jonathan Silver. He took possession of it a month later and immediately set to work improving both the exterior and the interior.

Although various activities took place at the mill, the enterprise which first put it and the village of Saltaire on the map did not open until Monday, November 2, 1987. Within two years, the 1853 Hockney Gallery was attracting public interest and international publicity from Melbourne to Los Angeles.

With typical panache, the 37-year-old Silver celebrated the opening of the world's first gallery dedicated to the works of his friend David Hockney with a champagne reception for hundreds of guests including the artist's 87-year-old mother Laura and other members of the family.

The 10,000 sqft. rectangular former spinning room contained 56 paintings, prints and drawings, mostly hung from former steam pipes. The scent of fresh flowers arrayed in an assortment of exotic vases and the sound of classical music filled the air. Silver was in his ele-

**That's my boy..mum is wowed by display**
*by John Hewitt*

DAVID HOCKNEY's 87-year-old mother Laura walked into an art exhibition yesterday and was astonished to find works by Bradford's top international artist hanging from overhead heating pipes.

**WORKS OF ART:** *Jonathan Silver with some of the Hockney paintings he helped bring to Salts Mill*

ment. Nearly ten years later, on September 25, 1997, Jonathan Silver died from cancer after a two-year battle. His wife Maggie, daughters Zoë and Davina, and brother Robin spoke at a commemorative celebration of his life before an invited audience of 500 at the mill on Sunday, December 14. David Hockney, the poet Tony Harrison, Sir Ernest Hall, Jonathan's former business partner at Dean Clough, Halifax, and concert pianist, also made contributions. The guests could take stock of the mill's development in the decade of Jonathan's ownership, and how the success of his particular kind of economic regeneration, a mixture of culture and commerce, had benefited Saltaire. The celebration took place in the third Hockney Gallery, for more pictures by the Bradford-born artist had been acquired over the ten years. Dinner was served in Jonathan's American-style Diner, the walls of which were covered

**Continued on Page 149**

John Boynton Priestley was born at 34 Mannheim Road, Manningham, which he himself describes as an "extremely respectable" suburb of Bradford. His father was a headmaster, the son of an illiterate mill worker; Priestley's mother died when he was two years old. He was educated at Whetley Lane Primary School and, with the help of a scholarship, Belle Vue Grammar School in Manningham Lane. But school bored him and when he left at sixteen he went to work ( from 1910–1914) as a junior clerk at Helm & Co., a wool firm in Bradford's grand Swan Arcade. So enamoured was he with the arcade that he titled the first part of his literary reminiscences, *Margin Released* (1962), 'The Swan Arcadian'. While at Helm & Co. (1910–1914), he joined the Labour Party and started writing after work; he had articles published in the *Bradford Pioneer*, the *Yorkshire Observer* and in London newspapers.

Bradford and its cityscape was to feature prominently in much of his work after he moved south, not least *Bright Day* and *When We Are Married*. In later life he campaigned against the mindless destruction of Bradford's Victorian buildings such as the glorious Swan Arcade demolished in 1962 to be replaced by the usual anonymous Brutalist box of glass and concrete.

In the *Heaton Review* (1931) he describes hometown Bradford as

> Not really a town at all; it is a vast series of pictures, in time and space; it is an autobiographical library; it is a hundred thousand succeeding states of mind; it is my childhood and youth; it is a lost world…Bradford itself is ugly and forbidding, and yet within the easiest reach…is some of the loveliest country in England.

The picaresque *The Good Companions* (1929) finds the aging, discontented Jess Oakroyd languishing in the Yorkshire town of Bruddersford (Bradford + Huddersfield). He decides to up and go, to leave his family and seek adventure "on t'road". Priestley uses dialect for all non-received pronunciation speakers of English throughout the novel. Jess heads south down the Great North Road.

The University of Bradford awarded Priestley an honorary Doctor of Letters in 1970, and he was awarded the Freedom of the City of Bradford in 1973. His connections with the city can also be seen in the J. B. Priestley Library at the University of Bradford, which he officially opened in 1975, and by 'the larger-than-life statue of him', commissioned by the Bradford City Council after his death, and which now stands in front of the National Media Museum.

Priestley's real love was for the Yorkshire Dales, of which he, a veteran global traveller, writes

> 'For variety of landscape these Dales cannot be matched on this island or anywhere else. A day's walk among them will give you almost everything fit to be seen on this earth.'
> (From his Introduction to *The Beauty of Britain* (1935).

Two years after his death in 1984 the ashes of JB Priestley were scattered in the St. Michael and All Angels churchyard in Wensleydale's Hubberholme. He described Hubberholme as *'one of the smallest, pleasantest places in the world'* (*The Other Place*, 1953). The church is next to the wonderful 17th century largely un-modernised George Inn – a favourite Priestley refuge. Elsewhere, he described Hubberholme as 'Hubberholme – just bridge, an inn and a church, all old – is sheer magic, not quite in this world' (*Life International*, 1966).

JB Priestley painting in the Dales near Ribblehead.
*photo Marie Hartley © Dalesman Publishing Company*

Bradford Corporation Tramways operated trams in the city from 1882 until 1950 and trolleybuses from 1911 until 1972. The first section of single-line track tram line on Manningham Lane started in September 1881. The finished line ran from Rawson Square in the city centre to Lister Park Gates. The horse-drawn service ran at 8 am on 2nd February 1882; the first additional line opened on 8th August 1882 along Leeds Road to Stanningley and was operated using steam traction because of the gradients involved. In 1896 electric trams were introduced. After the Second World War, the remaining tram lines were closed, and the last Bradford tramcar (No. 104) returned to Bankfoot depot for the last time on 6th May 1950.

A demonstration of kitchen appliances at Busby's department store in the 1950s at which hats were, of course, *de riguer*. The photographer seems to be attracting more interest 'though than the kitchen appliances. Busby's was one of two Bradford high street giants – this one on Manningham Lane. It was founded by Ernest Busby on Kirkgate in 1908 with forty staff, but by the '50s the store was keeping 830 people in work. Busby's closed their Kirkgate store on Easter Sunday 1930 to make the big move to Manningham Lane. The building exuded Victorian Gothic and the logo – four marching and helmeted Coldstream guards – became a badge of Bradford itself. The popular bargain basement rubbed shoulders with the showrooms full of luxury gowns and dresses… and furs. Ernest Busby was himself a furrier and bought in skins from Leipzig even before the first war. One mink coat sold for £4,600. Debenhams bought the business in August 1958. The store closed in 1978. In addition to the usual fare Busby's could boast a nail bar in the early 1960s.

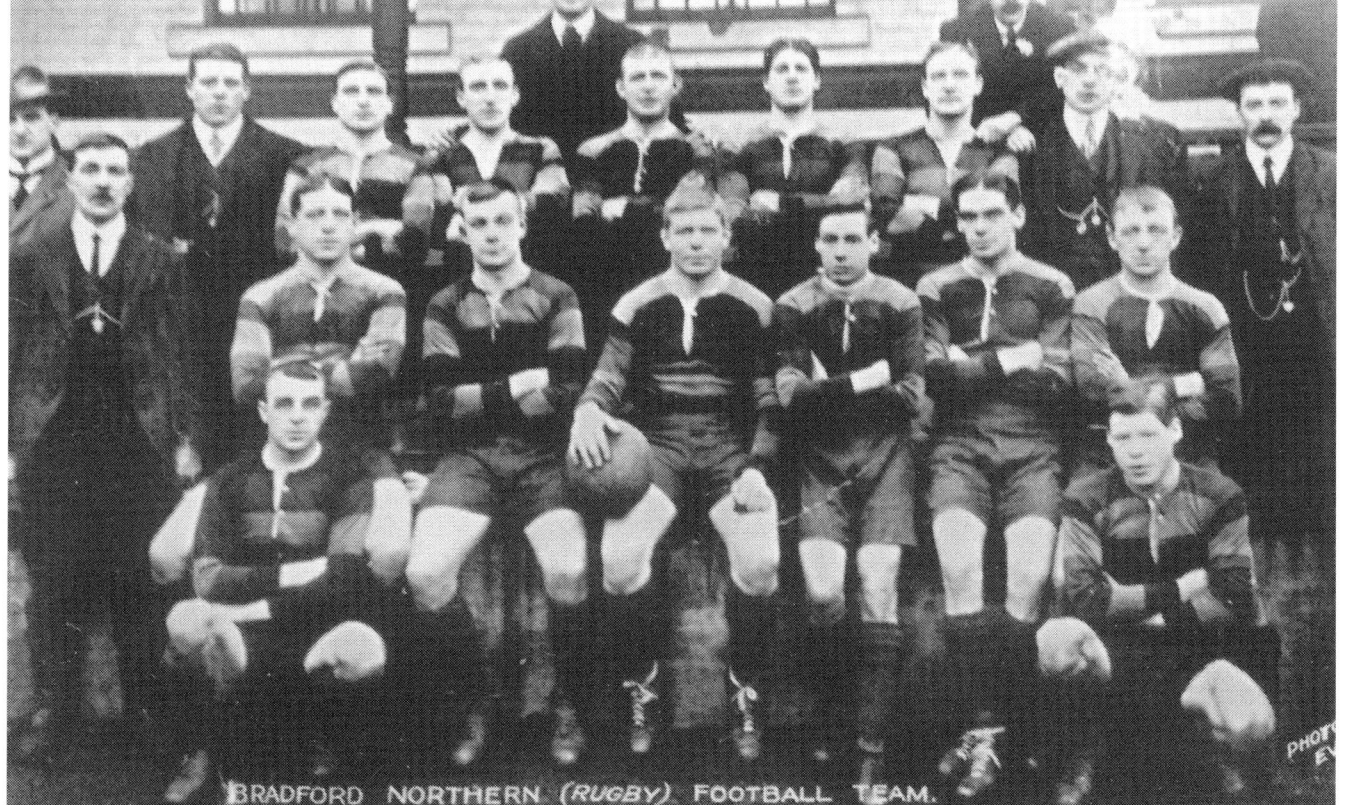

Bradford Northern Rugby Football Team started as The Bradford Football Club which was formed in 1863. Park Avenue became their home ground in 1880. The club's first major success came by winning the Yorkshire Cup in 1884. In 1895, along with neighbours Manningham F.C., Bradford was among the 22 clubs to secede from the Rugby Football Union after a meeting at the George Hotel in Huddersfield, over a dispute over "broken time" payments to players. These 22 clubs then formed the Northern Rugby Union. Manningham ran into financial difficulties and, despite a summer archery contest that raised enough money to ensure their survival, its members were persuaded to change to association football. The club was invited to join the Football League in 1903 as the newly renamed Bradford City AFC.

In 1933 Bradford Northern signed a ten-year lease with Bradford Council for a former quarry being used as a waste dump at Full House Top. It was converted into the biggest stadium outside Wembley. Ernest Call, the Director of Cleansing for Bradford City Council devised a system of controlled tipping that saw 140,000 cart loads of household waste deposited to form the characteristic banking at Odsal. In 1995, the Rugby League announced the formation of the Super League; the club's name was changed from Bradford Northern to Bradford Bulls. The league consisted of ten clubs from the existing First Division (including Bradford Bulls) plus London Broncos from the Second Division, and new club Paris Saint-Germain.

The stadium's highest attendance was 102,569 in 1954 for the Warrington-Halifax Challenge Cup Final replay, and for a domestic, non-final, Rugby League match, 69,429 at the third round Challenge Cup tie between Bradford Northern and Huddersfield in 1953. In early 2017 the Bulls were liquidated; on 1st September 2019, the club played their last game at Odsal. The Bulls left Odsal for a ground share with Dewsbury.

Manningham Mill Ladies' football team in 1921. On April 13th that year, in front of a crowd of about 12,000, Lister Ladies played the redoubtable Dick, Kerr Ladies, one of England's earliest women's teams and lost 0-6. Women's football was doing very nicely during and just after the First World War, until that is the hoary old suits in the Football Association imposed a ban on women playing in FA accredited grounds, a mean-spirited ban which extended from 1921 to 1971. Result: the end of women's football for 50 years and the own goal to end all own goals by the FA.

Women's teams and women's matches had clearly shown that they could attract huge crowds; for example, on Boxing Day, 1920 a crowd of 53,000 attended Goodison Park (and a further 14,000 were locked out) for a game involving the Dick, Kerr team against St Helens Ladies that raised £3,115 for the benefit of injured ex-servicemen for hospital funds. The crowd was the second largest ever recorded for any association game in England. Women's teams were spearheaded by the munitions workers during the war: the Dick, Kerr team, made up of employees of the Dick, Kerr munitions factory in Preston was formed in 1917 when fourteen women's teams entered the new Munitionettes Cup competition, the first to cater solely for women's football.

Manningham Mills Ladies team was soon followed by Hey's Brewery Ladies; Manningham Mills and Hey's Brewery also ran women's cricket teams. Dick, Kerr was later known as English Electric.

**HEY'S BREWERY (BRADFORD) LADIES' A.F.C.**
RECORD 1921-22. WINNERS YORKSHIRE LADIES' CHAMPIONSHIP, WHITEHEAD LIFEBOAT SHIELD, FIVE-A-SIDE YORKSHIRE TOURNAMENT. TWO DRAWN GAMES WITH DICK KERR'S FOR ENGLISH LADIES' CHAMPIONSHIP.

The ladies team at J Hey & Co. Ltd, Northbrook Brewery, Wilson Square, Lumb Lane. Hey & Co was built about 1861 as the Manningham Brewery for Clement Taylor & Son who had previously brewed at the Springhead Brewery, White Abbey, from 1853. Registered January 1898. It was acquired by Samuel Webster & Sons Ltd of Halifax in 1966 with 75 pubs.

Mr Graham Coates, a member of the brewing staff at Hey's from 1953-1966, apart from a two year break at Thwaites of Blackburn ending in 1959.

Joseph Hey and his batchelor uncle, William, went into business under the title W & J Hey, merchants of ale and porter, and bottlers, in 1874.

Hey's first brewery, previously known as the Springwell Brewery, then called the Northbroook Brewery, Bolton Road, Bradford, came into being as a brewhouse for the Draymen's Hotel.

*Industries of Yorkshire*, in 1888 gave the following description of Henry Harper's brewery:-

The premises consist of buildings two and five stories high (the tower), measuring 250 feet long and 50 broad, and equipped with all the most approved appliances, forming what is known as an eight quarter plant. Town and spring water was available, machinery included a steam engine, fired by a Cornish boiler. In the paved yard, beneath which cellars extended, were stables and a cask wash house.

A typical brewing day saw mashing commence at 4:30 am. Two mash tuns of 15 quarters and 12 quarters were employed. The liquor came from the city main… The firm employed a cooper and an apprentice in later years, to make and repair casks. Nine gallon kegs were used for the company's keg bitter and a few aluminium casks for draught ales. Around 600 barrels were produced a week, out of this roughly 160 went for bottling. From 1960, keg bitter sold 30 to 40 barrels a week and draught beer sold at a ratio of three of bitter, to two of mild with about two thirds of the mild brewed being dark.

After sterilization processing, beer for bottling was taken by tanker to the former West Riding Bottling Company's premises a short distance away at Elmsall Street.

Just prior to takeover, Heys were opening new public houses. When the brewery closed in January 1967, they owned around 75 houses. Many of their former pubs retain their "House of Heys" windows, some advertising Gold Cup or Victory Ale etched on the glass and originally painted. Most of their houses were in Bradford.

*- by Malcolm Toft,*
*http://breweryhistory.com/wiki/index.php*
*?title=Joseph_Hey_%26_Co_Ltd*

Wibsey was an important market village and has its own horse fair every year on 5th October. Fair Road has a funfair site, established for many generations. It is thought that the monks of Kirkstall Abbey started the fair in the 12th or 13th century; the first record is a reference in a dispute between former Lords, William Rookes and John de Lacy, to the "Revey Cross, sett up and standing at Revey Nabbe" where a fair was held. This would place the fairground near modern-day Buttershaw estate, where roads entitled "Reevy" exist today. By the mid 19th century the fairground was at or near its present site, hence Fair Road.

The Laughter Makers from Idle.

Gracie Fields outside Cartwright Hall Art Gallery promoting an Essex Terraplane Six. This was made by the Hudson Motor Company of Michigan, USA between 1932 and 1938. The sales slogan for the brand was "On the sea that's aquaplaning, in the air that's aeroplaning, but on the land, in the traffic, on the hills, hot diggity dog, THAT'S TERRAPLANING".

C Pullam Coal & Lime Merchant, Apperley Bridge about 1912.

The cluttered burial ground and the parsonage about 1910: *'a graveyard so filled with graves that the rank weed and coarse grass scarce had room to shoot up between the monuments'*. The three Brontë sisters were born at 74 Market Street in Thornton on the edge of Bradford. The remains of the church where their father preached, known as the Bell Chapel, can be seen in the restored old graveyard off Thornton Road opposite the current church. In 1820 their father was appointed to the perpetual curacy in Haworth seven miles away and moved with the family into the five-roomed Haworth Parsonage.

Fred Cecil Jones was born in Bradford in 1891, the son of artist Maud Raphael Jones, and studied at Bradford College of Art, 1915-16, and also part-time at Leeds College of Art. In 1916 Fred volunteered for the Army; he served as a reconnaissance artist, where he earned the nickname, 'Detail Jones', for the quality of his work like this painting of Thackley.

John Braine (1922 –1986), one of the so-called 'angry young men' of the fifties, was born in a pokey terraced house off Westgate in Bradford, and moved to Thackley when his father took a job at Esholt Sewage Works. Thackley was next door to grim and industrial Shipley, a Joe Lampton kind of town, *"where the snow seemed to turn black almost before it hit the ground"*. After time spent as junior salesman in Christopher Pratt's furniture shop and then as progress chaser at the Hepworth & Grandage piston factory, Braine worked as a library assistant in Bingley Library until 1942. He is most famous for his first novel, *Room at the Top* (1957), although he did write more, including its sequel *Life at the Top, The Crying Game* (1968) and *Writing a Novel* (1974), a guide for aspiring novelists.

The photo shows the business premises of Alfred Coe at 2 Barkerend Road. He was born at Undercliffe in February 1851, the son of Bridget and John Coe, whose occupation is given as clothier on Alfred's birth certificate. Alfred's trade is listed on the birth certificate of his third child born in 1879 as warp twister. Alfred established the Coe Collotype Company, turning out local postcards, one of the earliest series being 'The Old Bradford Series' some of which are featured in this book. The set first appeared in late 1902; they show sepia reproductions of the well known series of watercolour paintings by N.S. Crichton and Arthur North showing Bradford and its many characters during the latter part of the 19th century.

The Manningham Stocks – one of the cards in Coe's Old Bradford Series.

> Where St Paul's Church and St Paul's Road now stand there was an open space, called Stocks Green, adjoining Helliwell's Farm...[The stocks] were placed at the end of a footpath leading to the farmhouse... Comparatively recently the latter were removed from Stocks Green
> *William Cudworth, Histories of Manningham, Heaton and Allerton: Townships of Bradford. (Bradford, 1896). pp. 3*

Coe also published comic cards, including a whole series issued at the time of the Boer War entitled 'South African Fashion Plates'. 'The Continental Series' and 'The Publication Series'. These were based on a pun on words, for example 'America – A-Merry-Cur': the card depicts a dog with a bowler hat, cane bow tie and a glass of beer. Also, 'Australia -Hos-Trail-Yur?': a man being pulled on a rope behind a horse being dragged through a cactus. Other prominent local postcard publishers include Percy Lund, Humphries & Co., M. Field, T.M. Woodhead and Appleton & Co.

Tom Green's Refreshment House.

Joseph A. Hey Ltd – funeral directors and monumental masons. Herbert Hey is standing to the left of their special stagecoach at their Great Horton Road premises.

The meat section at Rawson Place Market.

Idle was a separate village as part of the Manor of Idle to the north east of Bradford; nowadays urban creep has reduced it to a suburb. The Manor comprised such hamlets as Buckmill and Wrose, and was bounded by the River Aire in the north and, in the east, Pighill Beck (now Haigh Beck) up to Blakehill Tongue.

Coal and stone were early Idle industries; stone was exported by way of the canal and later on the railway. Mills in the Idle area include Old Green Mill, Butt Lane Cotton Mill, Union Mills, Simpson Green Mill or Castle Mill, New Mill and Albion Mill. The last is seen in ruins in the photograph, a result of a fire on the 10th March 1911. The cause of the fire was unclear but the timbers of the mill were reportedly saturated with oil after years of wool processing. The fire caused considerable concern due to the proximity of the Airedale Gas Company's works but the gas was withdrawn and a greater disaster averted.

Idle used to be part of the parish of Calverley but in 1584 a chapel of ease was built on Town Lane and later in 1630 rebuilt on the same site. The building is now known as Old Chapel. A school was added which in 1836 was rebuilt as Round Steps School. The school building contained a lockup and the town's official offices, and was also used by the Mechanics' Institute. It was demolished in the late 19th century. In 1914 there was a move to demolish Old Chapel as well, to widen the road: a successful campaign to oppose this saved it.

The Idle Picture Palace opened in 1912 on The Green; it closed in 1959. Jowett Cars Ltd had a car factory in Bradford Road until 1954 when they sold the factory to International Harvester who turned out tractors there until the early 1980s.

The Idle Workingmen's Club is what Idle is world famous for. It was established in 1928, and seen here at that grand opening, by local sewage workers whose shifts and the pub licensing hours left them unable to have a drink after work. The unique name has acquired the club a cult status around the world, with much clamouring for an official 'Idle Working Men's Pass'. The membership exceeds 1,000; women were allowed to become members in 1995. The club has benefited by granting honorary memberships to people who would not normally fit its criteria for membership. Some current honorary members include Paul Gascoigne, Uri Geller, Roger Moore, Tom O'Connor and Lester Piggot. Richard Whiteley and Michael Jackson were also honorary members. In addition to the club there are over a dozen public houses and bars in Idle.

Locally, musical groups include the Idle and Thackley Operatic Society and the Idle Bell Ringers. The Idle Beer Festival is held at the Hepworth and Idle Cricket Club.

A Bradford Council employee hard at work in Idle's Town Lane. He's supposed to be overseeing the work of the Street Improvements Committee; outside Wilkinson's the florists in 1916.

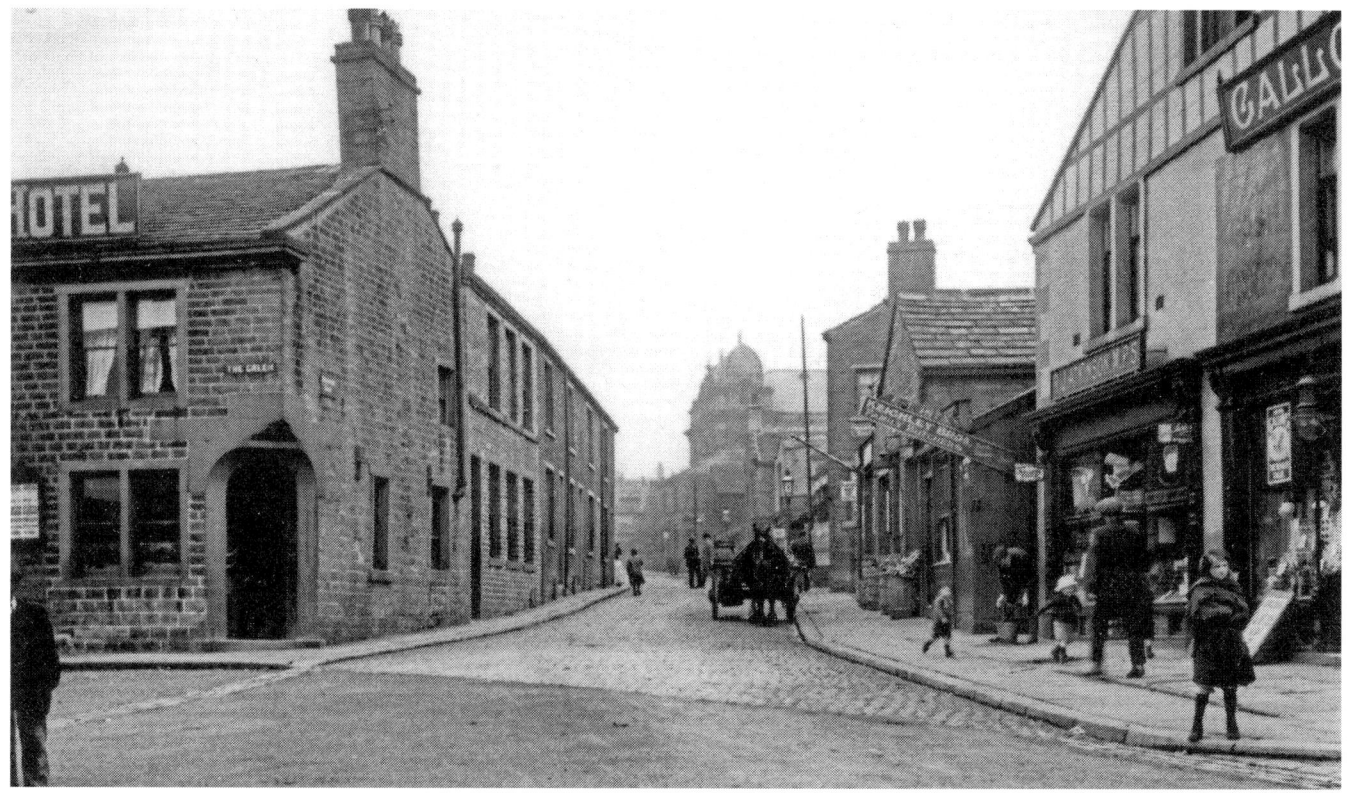

The pub just out of shot on the left is the Springfield Hotel at 179 Bradford Road.

Looking towards the Green along Bradford Road. Other Idle pubs include: Alexander (49 Albion Road); Brewery Tap (51 Albion Road); Hitching Post (54 Leeds Road); Idle Beerhouse (7 Albion Road); Idle Draper, (28 The Green); Lane Ends, (161 Norman Lane); White Bear, (41 High Street); White Swan, The (22 The Green); Balloon & Basket (Highfield Road); Coniston (Louisa Street); Shoulder of Mutton (589 Leeds Road).

Whit Monday Service On The Green, Idle, 1913.

Esholt village is 5 miles north of Bradford and has ecclesiastical origins, having been owned in the 12th century by Syningthwaite Priory, and Esholt Priory, a Cistercian nunnery dedicated to St Mary and St Leonard established at Lower Esholt.

The Esholt smithy. Between 1912 and 1915 Nanson, Barker & Co manufactured the Tiny cyclecar in Esholt. From 1919 they made larger cars under the Airedale brand but went into liquidation in 1924. A cyclecar was a small, lightweight and inexpensive car, the purpose of which was to fill a gap in the market between the motorcycle and the motor car. Cyclecars were propelled by engines with a single cylinder or V-twin configuration (or occasionally a four cylinder engine), which were often air-cooled. Sometimes motorcycle engines were used, in which case the motorcycle gearbox was also fitted. All cyclecars were required to have clutches and variable gears. But by the early 1920s, the cyclecar was doomed. Mass producers, such as Ford, were able to undercut the prices of the usually small cyclecar makers. Affordable cars such as the Citroën 5CV, Austin 7 or Morris Cowley were now available.

Apperley Bridge is north-east of Bradford on the Leeds and Liverpool Canal and the River Aire. Apperley Bridge railway station was situated across the boundary in Rawdon from 1846 to 1965. Woodhouse Grove School, whose land had been crossed by the railway. was an important customer in 1849; the railway agreed to purchase gas from the school to light the station. The railway was widened to four tracks in about 1900, taking more land from Woodhouse Grove School, who used the money to build a swimming baths. Steps were needed to board trains on platform 4.

Cottingley derives its name from the Cota or Cotta family and so means meadows of the sons of Cota. "Ing" being wood, "ley" field. Alternatively, "ting" or "ding" might mean moot or court here. There is another Cottingley in Leeds.

Bradford's Cottingley is famous for its fairies: the Cottingley Fairies feature in five photographs taken by Elsie Wright (1900–88) and Frances Griffiths (1907–86), two cousins; Sir Arthur Conan Doyle, a spiritualist, used them to illustrate an article on fairies in the Strand Magazine as evidence of psychic phenomena. In the early 1980s Elsie and Frances admitted that four of the photographs were fakes – they had used cardboard cut outs from a children's book, but Frances insisted that the fifth photograph was genuine.

Saltaire was established in 1851 and is the creation of Sir Titus Salt (1803-1876), a prominent industrialist in the woollen industry. Saltaire is a conflation of 'Salt' and 'Aire', the river on which the town stands. Salt moved his mills from Bradford, consolidating it all on this site so as to be close to the Leeds and Liverpool Canal and the Midland Railway. Salt believed that his commercial success was entirely God-given. At six storeys high and 180 yards long and with a floor space of over eleven acres, the ergonomic mill was the biggest and most modern in Europe.

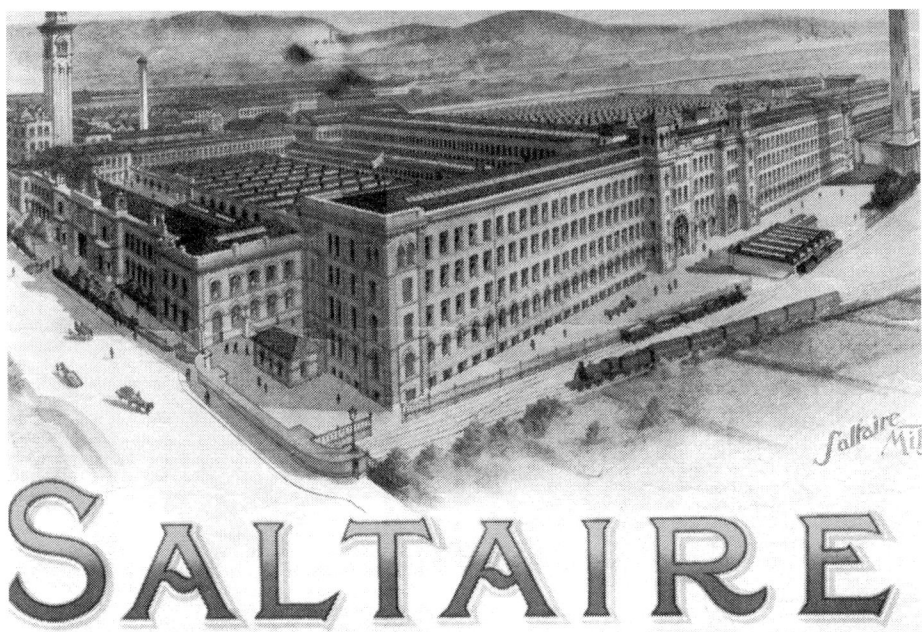

# SALTAIRE

On the left Simon Palmer's striking watercolour of Titus Salt surveying his Saltaire in an *Alice and Wonderland* type scene, complete with huge timepiece and adoring residents. A Simon Palmer watercolour below neatly captures Salt's well-known dislike of the public display of washing, showing a remorseful housewife, after being rebuked by Salt.
*both courtesy of and © Margaret Silver and Simon Palmer*

Output exceeded 30,000 yards of cloth per day; the weaving shed housed an incredible 1,200 power looms. Noise, and industrial injuries, were reduced by locating much of the machinery underground. Large flues removed smoke, dust and dirt from the atmosphere and from the factory floor. Fire safety equipment was state of the art. The heavily subsidized canteen was supplemented with facilities for workers to bring in their own food and cook on site. The impressive campanile must be one of the most aesthetic chimneys ever to be built. It is based on the campanile on the Basilica Santamaria Gloriosa in dei Frari in Venice. That campanile, the second tallest in the city after San Marco's, was completed in 1396. Titian is buried in the Frari. Salt's campanile was a worthy effort to maintain the character and pleasant atmosphere of Victoria Road.

Shelf is a village halfway between Bradford and Halifax. Domesday Book has it as Scelf; the name derives from the Anglo Saxon word 'Scelf', a broad and level shelf of land. Bradford Tramways Company (later the Bradford Tramways and Omnibus Company) were awarded the lease to run the trams in Bradford. A line was constructed in 1884 from the Town Hall Square to Shelf, together with a branch line from Odsal to Wyke. Although the Bradford Tramways and Omnibus Company was offered the operating lease, it was not really interested. The Corporation therefore invited offers; the lease for this new line was awarded to the newly formed Bradford and Shelf Tramways Company for 19 years.

The industrial model village of Ripley Ville grew out of the lamentable conditions in which workers were obliged to toil and live during the Industrial Revolution and much later. The villages were a culmination, generally speaking, of a growing awareness that something had to be done about the overcrowding and the unsanitary, disease-ridden houses and squalid streets which droves of workers left each dawn for the inhumane factory conditions and relentless labour which paid their meagre wages. The industrial village concept, however, was never just a question of altruism, philanthropy or paternalism. The welfare could never exist without the business, and profitable business at that: the

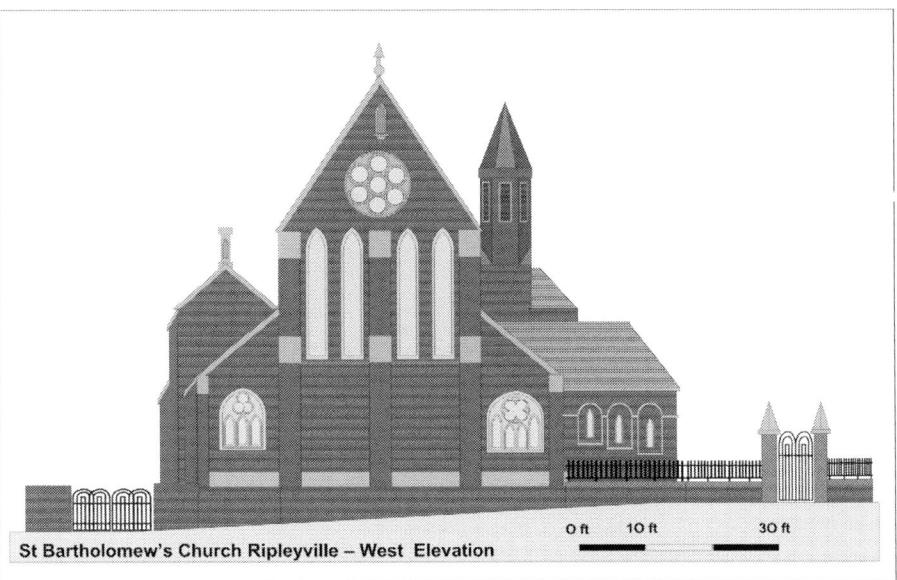

difference between the industrialist who built his model village and the average factory owner was that the benefactor felt the need to reinvest his profits for the betterment of his workers while at the same time benefitting from a stable, more productive, comparatively happy workforce.

*The image shows St Bartholomew's church Ripley Ville west elevation.*
*Scale drawing created in Visio from old photograps and plans by Peter Eltham*
*GNU Free Documentation Licence, Version 1.2 or any later version; Creative Commons share alike.*

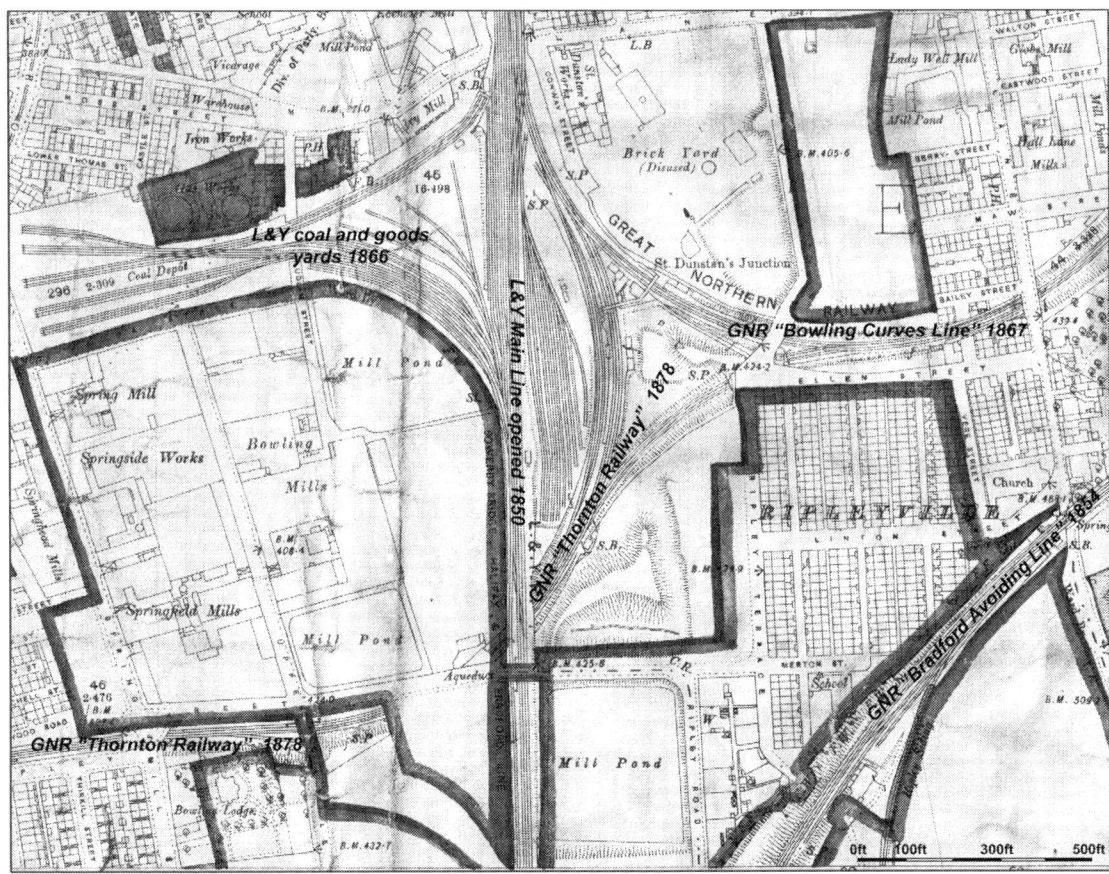

So, in 1866 industrialist, politician and philanthropist Henry William Ripley issued a prospectus for the construction of 300 "Working-men's dwellings" on his own land: four-bedroom through houses with rear yards and front gardens and an internal WC. These houses were to be sold to small landlords and owner occupiers. Lighting, ventilation, heating, storage, privacy and open space were taken into consideration and the design of the Ripley Ville houses incorporated these enhanced standards, and in a number of ways exceeded them.